WINNING
THE
WEEK

A simple yet powerful method to feel successful at the end of the week, regardless of what the week throws your way! Demir and Carey will radically change the way you approach your time management and teach you to plan for success.

— **Dr. Marshall Goldsmith**, Thinkers50 #1 Executive Coach and *New York Times* Best-Selling Author of *Triggers, Mojo,* and *What Got You Here Won't Get You There*

For professionals who are serious about attaining work-life balance, *Winning the Week* is full of practical tips that will help you work smarter, breathe calmer, and be more successful in your endeavors.

— **Dorie Clark**, *Wall Street Journal* Best-Selling Author of *The Long Game* and executive education faculty at Duke University Fuqua School of Business

Demir and Carey Bentley are laser-focused on techniques that work in the real world. Drawing on their experience after coaching thousands of clients, you'll learn their simple framework you can use to get exponential results. Read *Winning the Week* to learn from two of the best in the industry.

— **Preston Smiles**, international Best-Selling Author, serial entrepreneur, and master coach

Getting it all done and getting burned out in the process is the antithesis of success! *Winning the Week* shows you how to be more productive, more calm, and more successful in your workweek.

— **JJ Virgin**, four-time *New York Times* Best-Selling Author and celebrity nutrition and fitness expert

WINNING

THE

HOW TO PLAN A SUCCESSFUL
WEEK, EVERY WEEK

WEEK

DEMIR and CAREY BENTLEY

NEW YORK
LONDON • NASHVILLE • MELBOURNE • VANCOUVER

WINNING THE WEEK

How to Plan a Successful Week, Every Week

Published in New York, New York, by Morgan James Publishing. Morgan James is a trademark of Morgan James, LLC. www.MorganJamesPublishing.com

Proudly distributed by Publishers Group West®

A **FREE** ebook edition is available for you or a friend with the purchase of this print book.

CLEARLY SIGN YOUR NAME ABOVE

Instructions to claim your free ebook edition:
1. Visit MorganJamesBOGO.com
2. Sign your name CLEARLY in the space above
3. Complete the form and submit a photo of this entire page
4. You or your friend can download the ebook to your preferred device

ISBN 9781636982748 paperback
ISBN 9781636982755 ebook
Library of Congress Control Number: 2023942589

Cover Design by:
Laura Patricelli
www.designmastermind.com

Interior Graphics by:
Harlee Keller

Morgan James is a proud partner of Habitat for Humanity Peninsula and Greater Williamsburg. Partners in building since 2006.

Get involved today! Visit: www.morgan-james-publishing.com/giving-back

For hard workers who need more breathing room
to chase their dreams

CONTENTS

INTRODUCTION

It's 6:15 on a Friday night, and you're coming home at the end of a hard week...

Not the kind of week where all the lights turned green and everyone laughed at your jokes, but sadly a regular kind of week, where you tried to spin all the plates and some of them crashed to the floor. You've been through the wringer, and let's be honest: it shows. Trudging through the front door, you drop your bags and toss your keys onto that little shelf with a mirror (technically, it's called the foyer mirror). You can't help but catch a glimpse of yourself in that mirror, with tired eyes but bravely holding it together. Then you swiftly move on because it's Friday night, damn it, and you're determined to get as much "happy time" as possible. Bring on the Chardonnay!

But wait. Something happened there, and you missed it. Rewind the tape.

That glance into the mirror was the critical dividing line between your work life and your personal life. Let's pause right here and give this moment its due. What did you see when you looked at yourself in the mirror? It's natural to look a little haggard because the week was a battle. But did you feel like you were the winner of that battle, lending your struggle dignity and purpose? Or were you the loser, returning home under a cloud of shame and self-doubt?

I playfully call this the Foyer Mirror Test. That moment when you enter through the door and set down your keys, you are at a critical fork in the road: This is where you decide whether you won the week or lost it.

For most people this happens unconsciously, but this tiny decision has monumental ramifications. If you decide that you were victorious, you go on to treat yourself like a hero returning from a glorious battle. Putting your phone on its charger, you eagerly embrace home life. You change into comfy clothes and blast your favorite playlist. Pouring a glass of wine, you toast to yourself, and that first sip is pure celebration. Despite the exhaustion (or maybe because of it), there's a sense of accomplishment and pride. If you think about work at all, it's to exult in your victory and possibly brag to your partner. Feeling genuine closure on the week, you give yourself permission to become a person again, not just some employee on the eighteenth floor. This is the best version of yourself at the end of a week, and if this were how we all felt on Friday, the world would be a much better place.

Sadly, this isn't the way this story goes most of the time. There's a "defeated version" that goes more like this:

That moment you look in the foyer mirror, you unconsciously decide that you lost the week. You can't put your finger on it, but a faint cloud of guilt and anxiety follows you around. You keep replaying scenes from the week in your mind—your brain's way of trying to get closure. But it's not working. Despite your best attempts to shake it off, you can't stop thinking about work—which is ironic because at work you couldn't focus on the task at hand for wanting to think about anything else. Now back at home, you're stuck in "work mode." You begin cooking dinner as if it's yet another problem to be solved, another obstacle to overcome. In fact, all of your interactions at home just seem like more problems, sucking the joy out of moments that should have been savored. Pouring your second glass of wine, you realize that you can't remember drinking the first one, much less enjoying it.

As a productivity coach, I have heard variations on this same story thousands of times. In the "victorious version" of the story, a person comes home, gets closure on work, and proceeds to enjoy their life. They genuinely feel restored after a weekend like this, and come Monday they're chomping at the bit to get back to work and tackle big problems.

But I'm sure you can guess that, more often than not, I hear the defeated version of this story. The version in which the person can't get closure on work, so they can't allow themselves to relax. Stuck in zombie mode, they feel the weekend slip by too fast. In the best-case scenario, they are able to force a smile and make a good show of it, but their heart isn't really in it. In the worst cases, these are the weekends when they wish they had a do-over. Either way, come Monday, they are exhausted. It doesn't take long to burn out when you're having week after week like this.

Having coached so many people on the front lines of their productivity battle, I've come to believe this is a nearly universal phenomenon. Every person has a moment, whether they detect it or not, when they decide whether they won their week or they lost it. And that decision determines whether they allow themselves to release the past and come fully into the present to enjoy their life.

THE CONQUEROR'S CURSE

Last year I was having lunch with a friend who was visiting me in Medellín, Colombia. Surrounded by oversized greenery, tropical flowers, and bird calls, my friend conceded, "You've got a pretty good life down here. But...isn't it draining to be constantly working with underachievers and burnouts?" I almost choked, then burst out laughing. Are my clients underachievers? A bunch of low-performing burnouts?

Quite the opposite. Most of my clients have stunning résumés, and they operate successful brands and growing businesses. They include executives at top tech companies and even famous Hollywood actors—people who have climbed to the heights of their profession.

No, people don't seek me out because they lack success. They seek me out because they aren't *enjoying* their success. In some cases, they are straining under the weight of success. These people have been winning big for the majority of their adult lives, *but that's precisely the problem*. Life has a way of loading you down as you climb to the top. We just collect more responsibilities: marriages, homes, kids, volunteer and work commitments. And a big life can weigh a lot. At the same time, we steadily lose the energy—and even the passion—that we once had—just when we need it the most!

This phenomenon is what I call the Conqueror's Curse: winning life's battles when you're young loads you down with more territory you have to defend as you get older. You're spread thin and fighting on multiple fronts, even as the energy you once had for the fight diminishes. If you knew how driven and independent my clients were, you'd understand what a bitter pill that is for them to swallow.

Some clients come to me because their progress in life has slowed to a halt. They know they have the potential to do more, but they are so loaded down with responsibilities, they can't seem to move an inch. In fact, they start to sense that the tide of the battle is shifting against them. Often the best they can do is mount a brave defense, keeping the enemy at bay to maintain their position for as long as possible. But any victories they have are quickly eclipsed by the sense that they are nevertheless (slowly) losing the war. Without that forward momentum, their valiant efforts just give way to frustration and defeatism.

Other clients come to me in denial that the tide had turned against them. They don't want to see that they are losing more weeks than they are winning. But deep down, they still feel it—that creeping sense of dread, the permanent low-grade anxiety—which means that, more often than not, they deny themselves permission to live their life to its fullest. This makes a twisted kind of sense because it's impossible to relax when it seems like the enemy is at your gates.

Worst by far are the clients I call "grinders." These are highly motivated individuals used to putting their head down and doing hard work. Their entire life, their superpower has been ignoring pain and just "getting the work done," but all the things they stuffed away in youth are now exploding like a volcano in midlife. I've seen the results firsthand, and it can be an ugly reckoning.

Let me ask you: Is this ringing any bells? Do you give it "your all" at work, but still feel like you're falling behind? Or do you feel trapped beneath your potential while all your energy is devoted to keeping your head above water? And because of that, are you denying yourself permission to enjoy your life?

NEARLY WORKING MYSELF TO DEATH

It sure rings bells for me, because I lived that life too.

In July of 2010, I was in the prime of my career. I had just been promoted and was now one of the youngest senior equity analysts on Wall Street. I was making regular television appearances on financial news networks like CNBC, Bloomberg TV, and Fox Business.

But instead of flying high, I was flat on my back (literally), recovering from surgery in a hospital bed. This was my second surgery to battle the runaway effects of an intense but mysterious autoimmune disorder. I'll spare you the gruesome details of how my digestive system went awry, but it wasn't pretty. I had tried hard to ignore it for as long as I could, hoping it would go away. But now it was affecting my work, taking me out for days or weeks at a stretch.

I wasn't a hotshot—I was a hot mess!

My doctors were puzzled by someone so young suddenly starting to see critical system failure. As happens so often in the case of autoimmune diseases, the doctors couldn't agree on a diagnosis. And the treatments they had tried weren't working. Finally, one doctor thought to ask me, "How many hours are you working, by the way?"

"Never less than eighty hours a week—sometimes as many as one hundred!" I bragged.

I wasn't remotely ashamed of my long work hours. Like many New Yorkers, it was a point of personal pride! In case you're not familiar, the work culture in New York City is brutal. They celebrate "hustle culture," a euphemism for brute-forcing your way to success by working around the clock. And I was a true believer in the cult of hard work. I worked nights and weekends all throughout my twenties and thirties. Even as I suffered consequences like ill-health, massive weight gain, and failed relationships, I knew it would eventually all pay off with interest.

But I was wrong. It didn't pay off. It landed me in the hospital, facing the risk of early death. And just like a believer losing faith in his religion, I felt betrayed and stupid and lost.

It's estimated that 24 million people in the United States currently have an autoimmune condition—which is about one in every fourteen people. That means a lot of folks you know are managing one of these nasty conditions every day. These strange diseases (like rheumatoid arthritis, psoriasis, Crohn's disease, and celiac disease) involve your immune system going into overdrive and attacking healthy cells in your body. In the very worst cases, entire systems can fail. Even in mild cases, these are chronic conditions, meaning that there is no "cure"—they will impact your quality of life for the rest of your life.

These conditions are often caused by stress. In a massive thirty-year study of over a million people, scientists from the University of Iceland found a strong link between psychological stress and physical inflammatory conditions. Individuals with high levels of stress—induced by trauma, lack of sleep, or overwork—were up to forty times more likely to develop an autoimmune disease.

After learning about my insane working hours, my doctors asked me about my stress levels (they were sky-high) and how much I was sleeping (not nearly enough). With those answers in hand, my three doctors finally converged on a diagnosis. Due to my chronic overworking, I was now at risk for "sudden occupational mortality," a condition where a young person who appears to be otherwise healthy dies prematurely from the stress of overwork. In plain language: I was working myself to death. Though it's not a common way to die in North America, it's well-known in Asian societies, going by the names *karoshi* in Japan, *gwarosa* in South Korea, and *guolaosi* in China.

My doctors' prescription was upsettingly simple. I was to immediately limit my working hours to no more than forty per week. For me, this felt like telling a professional basketball player, "You can keep playing, but you have to do it with one hand tied behind your back!" I was furious because this felt like an impossible limitation that would definitely spell the end of my career. Thankfully, once again I was very wrong. Those doctors set me on a path that changed my life forever.

THE AMERICAN DREAM—OR THE AMERICAN TREADMILL?

I'm not alone in getting carried away with working too much. We're suffering through a particularly difficult period when it comes to work-life balance.

Economists delight in data that shows that we aren't working any more hours than our parents' generation, or the generation before that. But when I tell my clients that, they are dumbfounded. My clients who have been working since the 1980s tell me that they have felt a dramatic increase in their working hours. And they aren't alone: 40 percent of workers feel that their workload has increased in the last three to five years. So what gives here? Have we just gotten weaker? Are we a bunch of whiners? As a practitioner working on the front lines, I find this data to be misleading to the point of gaslighting. Three trends are conspiring to disguise increased working hours and pressures.

First, in most families, both partners have to work in order to make ends meet. So even if both partners are working an "average" workweek, the fact that they are both working puts incredible strain on a family unit. A UK study of the impacts on family life found that families had to work in "shifts" to manage the load, with half of families unable to eat meals together most days. They found that only a minority of "dual income" families worked the standard nine-to-five hours. Instead, many of them were working a "second shift" after the kids went to bed at night to get everything done. This led to lower-quality family life, strained relationships, and higher divorce rates.

Second, technological advances have allowed us to bring work home, resulting in a disastrous invasion of our personal time. Knowing how bad this has become, most HR departments are careful to encourage employees to sign off at 5:00 p.m. But managers in these same companies send the exact opposite message, celebrating and promoting the employees who work around the clock. This creates a "race to the bottom" culture where people feel tremendous social pressure to work after hours if they want to advance their careers. A recent survey found that 92 percent of workers regularly work on evenings and weekends, with 40 percent of people being "always available" for their work. The only people who can put a stop to it—employers—have a strong disincentive to do so.

Finally, we're getting less "lifestyle" for our labor. The average American worker today is 400 percent more productive than a worker was in 1950. Theoretically, this means that one spouse should only have to work eleven hours per week to maintain the same standard of living that we enjoyed in 1950. Wouldn't that be nice? Instead, the opposite has happened. Again, economists claim that incomes have risen, so what are we complaining about? But current inflation measures fail to adequately account for the most significant markers of a middle-class lifestyle: owning a home and a car, having health coverage, and paying for childcare, education, and end-of-life care. The costs of these critical goods and services have exploded at a rate that far outpaces base inflation. Put simply, a middle-class lifestyle costs more than it used to, something that any first-time homebuyer in a major metropolitan area or anyone putting a kid through college could tell you.

This is the reality I felt working in finance in New York. Despite having a top-tier job, I saw no path to owning a home. Now, having coached thousands of people, this is the reality I see every day on the front lines. Even with two incomes, families are struggling to maintain the lifestyle that came much more easily to their parents' generation. That puts tremendous pressure on families and partners, pressure that threatens to break up families. At the same time, work has invaded every nook and cranny of our life—in some cases even our dreams!

ESCAPING OVERWORK

Within a week of my doctors' ultimatum, I went from working eighty hours a week to working forty hours a week. My symptoms completely subsided in less than two months, and I was feeling healthier than ever. And my work wasn't suffering. Far from it—I got a huge promotion! My health crisis ended up being the forcing function that helped me discover a way of working less while experiencing more success, happiness, and longevity. I call it The Winning The Week Method.

I used this method to rapidly advance my Wall Street career. Combining it with other productivity hacks, I eventually reduced my Wall Street work hours to just two a week. Wanting to see how far we could go, my wife, Carey, and I broke free of the rat race and ultimately achieved within five years what I call the Four Freedoms:

1. *Financial Freedom:* Starting $100,000 in debt, we became debt-free. A short time later, we hit our financial independence goal, which means we can retire whenever we choose. This financial freedom has radically changed our relationship to work. Today we work because we want to, not because we have to.

2. *Time Freedom:* In 2015, Carey and I committed to working less than thirty hours a week, and it's a promise we have kept religiously. Last year I averaged twenty-seven hours per week. That free time creates space for the good stuff in life, like working out, taking a nap, or just spending an afternoon on the couch listening to an album.

3. *Career Freedom:* With financial stability and excess time, Carey and I are able to focus on only the work we want to be doing. Safe to take bigger risks, we experienced career success that we never imagined possible. Today we get to work on things that inspire us and focus our efforts on the areas where we can do the most good.

4. *Spiritual Freedom:* Now that work no longer steals oxygen from the other important parts of our life, we've seen those other areas of our life blossom. We travel frequently with our daughter, take time for ourselves and each other, and have an active spiritual practice. In other words, we have time to be present for what's truly important in life.

For me, all of those freedoms came from one simple point of origin: getting organized and consistently winning my weeks. Given that relatively rapid transformation, I had to wonder: Why hadn't someone taught me this earlier in life? I hadn't had one class on productivity in high school, college, or the workplace. Why didn't anyone teach me how to manage my workload?

The answer is frightening: We can't teach it because we don't know it. We're all hanging on by a thread, just trying to keep it together.

Inspired by our experience escaping overwork and taking back our lives, Carey and I resolved to help other people get organized and do the same. We started our company, Lifehack Method, to teach people to take back control of their time and create the Four Freedoms in their own lives. We've helped over fifty thousand people, working with hotshots and average Joes alike. We've helped millionaire business owners and executives from big companies like Facebook, Google, Uber, and PepsiCo. But we've also worked with nonprofit executives, pastors, stay-at-home parents, and everyone in between. Our mission has been to help anyone suffering due to their workload and to show them how to create a powerful workflow, get back on offense, and see themselves progressing to their best life.

Knowing that we can't fit all of our methods into one book, our goal in this book is to offer the reader the keystone piece of our methodology, what we call The Winning The Week Method. This is what turned my life around when I was on the brink. It's a simple yet powerful framework for handling the strain of modern life with ease and without ever burning out. We've created an operating system for winning your week, every single week. This is something that anyone can implement right away to see transformative results but also forms the foundation upon which to build more advanced productivity skills. Carey and I are equal partners in every way, and we wrote this book together, but we have chosen to narrate in my (Demir's) first-person voice. It makes for easier reading and felt natural to us, given that I do most of the coaching on the front lines.

If you already know a bit about productivity but still feel like something is missing, this book will be right up your alley. I hope it will give you that "I know kung fu" moment where things finally click into place. If you're new to productivity, this book will provide you with a foundation to build on as you progress to more advanced techniques.

To be clear—I'm not promising you that everything will magically start going your way. Instead, I'm promising you a method to help you move the big things forward despite the obstacles and consistently stay on offense instead of defense. At the minimum, you'll find that this method will make your life easier and more enjoyable. Taken to the extreme, though, this method can lay the foundation for seemingly superhuman feats of productivity.

But be warned—this book is not a "flavor of the month" productivity fad. If fads were going to work, they would have worked already. This method is designed for people who are ready to buckle down and face this productivity problem head-on. If you have the courage to do that, I promise that when you look at yourself in the mirror on Friday night, you'll know that you won your week, and you won big. And come Monday morning, you'll be chomping at the bit to get back in the game.

Let's dive in.

PART 1

BUILD A
WINNING PLAN

1

WHY WIN THE WEEK?

I NOTICE THAT MANY OF MY CLIENTS UNCONSCIOUSLY USE BATTLE or war analogies when talking about their week. Maybe you find yourself saying things like:

"I'm dying here."

"I'm losing ground."

"I'm overwhelmed."

"I'm on defense, not offense."

"I'm winning the small battles but losing the war."

Let me suggest a better analogy for winning your weeks: a professional athlete playing their sport. Sport is an obvious proxy for war, but it's a far better analogue for work. Unlike war, in sports you can lose a lot of games and keep playing—because losing a game is not a death sentence. Even better, in sports no one is expected to win every game—you just need to win more than you lose to be considered a winner. The same goes for work.

That doesn't mean there aren't consequences in sports, though. There are moments when people get cut from the team or simply fail to progress to the next level. Like when a player's contract isn't renewed, or they don't make the cut moving from high school to college soccer. So in sports, there are severe consequences for one's performance. But everything isn't riding on the outcome of one game. The consequences are spread out over time, giving players space to learn and improve. Even if an athlete gets cut from the game altogether, they get to live on and play a different game that pays their bills. In that way, sport is a much more forgiving enterprise than war.

I'd like you to think of yourself as the star player playing the game of your life. Much as in sports, the consequences of winning or losing this week aren't life or death for you. You won't be loved or hated based on any single week of your game. And you can lose a lot of games/weeks and still make it to the playoffs of your career. Ironically, there's a lot of losing involved in winning, and even some winning involved in losing.

But in life, as in sports, there are real consequences for consistently poor performance in the medium and long term. You could get "benched," meaning your poor performance results in missing out on prime opportunities to shine. You could also get "cut from the team," as in getting fired or losing an opportunity to advance to the next level. And since we're all aging, we don't get the chance to hit reset and start over again. Some windows of opportunity that close will never be reopened.

I introduce this sports analogy because it's useful on multiple levels in explaining my approach to winning the week. I've come to see that a week is an ideal increment in which to tackle your productivity—one "game" in the tournament of your life. Why a week, and not a day, a month, or a quarter? Given how much I emphasize this increment of time, allow me to peel back some layers and explain why I think the weekly focus is so powerful.

REASON #1: IT MAPS WELL TO REAL LIFE

If you like the thought of approaching your work like a game, and you're looking to map that onto real life, the week is the obvious choice. A weekly cadence matches a rhythm that we already have built into the fabric of our society: the workweek and the weekend. You're already attuned to this rhythm in so many ways: you "start the game" on Monday morning, then continue making your plays and overcoming obstacles throughout the week. Then on Friday night, this week's game is over, and the weekend offers you a chance to reflect on whether you won or lost. After getting some rest, you start a new game again on Monday.

Where else in our world do you find a matching cadence of work and rest? Not monthly, or even quarterly. Possibly annually (with the holidays), but now we're talking about time increments that are too large and unmanageable. A week is large enough to accomplish a great deal, but small enough to generate lots of learning opportunities.

Think about how a soccer team continually improves. At practice, the players learn new strategies, which they try in a game. Afterward, they can rewatch the recording of the game and identify what went wrong, what went right, and what to work on in the following practice. Then it starts again from the beginning, except this time with better information. That's their feedback loop: practice, play, rewatch...practice, play, rewatch.

Now imagine a team that doesn't have a feedback loop in place. Sadly, I don't have to imagine this scenario, because when I was in high school, I was on the worst soccer team in our league. We got clobbered by every single school. Not for lack of trying—we practiced hard and truly wanted to win! But our coach didn't have a feedback loop in place, so despite our best efforts to improve, we kept making the same mistakes over and over again. Not only did we fail to improve—we actually got worse because we grew disheartened and frustrated, which opened the door to fatalism and a victim mentality.

This happens in our work too. Without an effective feedback loop, we keep making the same mistakes, growing frustrated, and even wanting to quit. But used properly, a weekly approach to tackling goals can become that powerful feedback loop, giving you regular chances to rest and reflect on how to improve. Each week can become an opportunity to try new things, evaluate your wins and losses, and fine-tune your approach. This kind of strategy results in small but very consistent incremental improvement. The compounding effect of those improvements quickly snowballs and becomes exceptional progress.

REASON #2: YOU CAN'T WIN EVERY DAY, BUT YOU CAN WIN EVERY WEEK

Expecting yourself to be perfect (or even good) every day is an impossible standard, because your performance will always vary. Even at your very best, the chaos of life will throw you curveballs. Why yoke yourself to that impossible expectation? I love playing to win the week because it means I don't have to be perfect every day. I can have lots of "bad days" and still win my week. I'll go even further: sometimes I feel like I got my butt kicked every single day, and yet I look back and realize that I won the week overall. Has that ever happened to you?

My client Alexis is a great example of this: she suffered from a bad case of perfectionism, pushing herself hard to grow her franchise business, even as she tried to be an exceptional mom to her three daughters. Her focus on being perfect every day had driven her to the edge of madness. I'm not kidding—there was a crazy look in her eyes when we first spoke. When I gave her permission to lose some days but still win the week, she immediately felt a sense of relief, almost like a weight had been lifted. At the same time, she started knocking down milestones that she'd been slipping on for over a year. Fast-forward eighteen months and her company had become one of

Inc. 500's fastest-growing franchises. When I caught up with her, I asked her what had changed. How had she become such a superstar?

She laughed, "What's funny, Demir, is that I still feel so sloppy. I definitely wouldn't want anyone to see me behind the scenes of any given day. But I have to admit, I'm way more relaxed. I'm not driving myself nearly as hard. And even though I'm still getting my butt kicked on some days, I'm winning nearly every week...nailing milestones and targets. I never feel perfect at any given moment, but when I look back on the last twelve months, I can't believe the difference in what I've accomplished. So I guess the results speak for themselves."

I find it significant that Alexis still describes herself as "sloppy" despite her transformation and unmistakable business success. This reveals something important about winning your week: it doesn't have to look pretty all the time to result in a win. In fact, it won't look pretty all the time.

A PRODUCTIVITY SYSTEM THAT DEMANDS PERFECTION IS INHERENTLY UNSUSTAINABLE.

@DEMIRANDCAREY

REASON #3: A WEEKLY APPROACH OFFERS MORE POTENTIAL PATHWAYS TO YOUR WIN

Another reason I like the idea of winning the week is that it opens up more pathways to a win. And the more potential routes you have to hit your goal, the more likely it is that you'll reach it—not to mention you'll feel less stress when one pathway is invariably blocked.

Flexible dieting is a great example of this effect in action. Flexible dieting means you get to eat anything you want, as long as it fits into your weekly calorie and macro targets. Although my identical twin brother had incredible success with flexible dieting for years, I resisted. I thought it required body-builder-like discipline. But finally, in the face of total failure after trying everything else, I broke down and tried it. To my surprise, instead of feeling rigid, I found that flexible dieting was…well, flexible.

I could make food choices that matched my mood, hunger, and environment each day. And all I had to do was make sure the total amount of protein, fats, and carbohydrates I consumed fit my target percentages by the end of the week. It's been years now, and I've found this approach to be sustainable and highly enjoyable, because the diet doesn't require perfection at every moment. I can make infinite food choices—even food "mistakes"—and still find a way to hit my targets and win my week.

A weekly workflow brings that same kind of flexibility to your productivity. You can have a bad moment or bad day and make up for it in another moment or on another day. You can take that walk when the sun is shining or ditch a few hours of work to spend time with your kid after they've had a rough day. In that way, there are infinite choices you can make and still win your week.

My client Catherine captured this feeling perfectly:

> There was an ease today that I haven't had in a LONG time. I was able to deal with a quick emergency trip to the doctor for my son's ear infection, be there for my eleven-year-old daughter when she had some drama with a friend, take a twenty-minute nap, and even take my dog for a walk. And I still got my number one priority done for the day. I was able to go make dinner without work anxiety hanging over my head. I am free for the rest of the evening and kind of feeling a bit lost. I'm not sure

how this is possible, but it's SO eye-opening. I've had a noose around my neck for years.

Wow...I have a sense of hopefulness that this is how my life can feel all the time. No doubt there are still hard days ahead, but I'm going to keep this one for the record books—how I aspire to feel every day!

Rather than hoping that everything will go well during your week, I invite you to expect that it won't. Pulling your focus out to winning the week allows you to flow around obstacles and bend with the chaos of your life. No matter how things go awry—and they will—you can navigate adverse circumstances and reach your final destination.

REASON #4: A WEEKLY APPROACH ENCOURAGES YOU TO SYNCHRONIZE YOUR PRODUCTIVITY SKILLS INTO A COHESIVE WHOLE

All too often new clients come to me obsessed with niche productivity topics. The hot topic seems to change every few months, depending on what the gurus say online. These same clients are annoyed (and rightly so) that their productivity isn't great, despite all the effort they put into executing these productivity fads over the years.

The reason they aren't seeing results is simple. When you follow these "flavor of the month" productivity fads, you lose sight of the larger picture of your *workflow*. Workflow is an idea that encompasses everything that has to happen for you to get your work done and move the ball forward: the disciplines, the mindsets, the techniques, the technologies, and the systems. I help move my clients away from productivity fads to a whole-systems approach, where the focus is synchronizing your productivity skills into a cohesive whole and getting the sensation of what it feels like when it's all working in harmony. This is an essential prerequisite for more advanced productivity practices—which is why so many folks get stuck. The tail is wagging the dog.

Think back to the first time you rode a bike. In the beginning it was overwhelming because it seemed like ten different skills: steering, pedaling, balancing, braking, navigating, and so on. You probably even crashed a couple times because it was so overwhelming. But eventually all of those skills synchronized until they became one integrated experience: simply riding the bike. Once you had that rhythm, the bike just felt like an extension of yourself. Even after years of not riding, many people can pick it right back up again.

In the same way, there's a "feel" to your workflow—a synchronization of disparate skills into one cohesive experience. You'll know you've had your breakthrough moment when you stop feeling like you're doing ten separate things at once and everything merges in a way that feels almost effortless. Once you have that "feel"—that muscle memory—it's impossible to lose, sort of like riding a bike. By zooming out to a weekly view of your productivity, the emphasis on your productivity shifts from the micro to the macro. Instead of obsessing over perfecting disconnected productivity techniques, a weekly approach begins to integrate them all into one workflow.

REASON #5: A WEEKLY APPROACH LEVERAGES THE POWER OF PARKINSON'S LAW

Have you ever noticed that when you're under the gun—facing a deadline—you can get a month's worth of work done in one week? But without that deadline, you could drag out a day's worth of work into a week or even more?

Cyril Northcote Parkinson famously wrote, "Work expands so as to fill the time available for its completion." Since then, Parkinson's law has become the best-known explanation for why we can take three months to write a twenty-page essay or miraculously finish it in just one day. The problem with Parkinson's law is that most of the time it works against us. Giving yourself three months to work on a project usually means you're going to do it the week before it's due. Ironically, giving yourself too much time to work on something can have precisely the opposite effect you intended.

The good news is that Parkinson's law can work powerfully in your favor. By cleverly playing with deadlines and setting a ceiling on the amount of time you're willing to spend on each project (also known as time boxing), you can create a sense of urgency that teases out your best performance. I find that a week is a good-sized chunk of time in which to take action on your biggest priorities. It's small enough that you don't procrastinate, but big enough to make a considerable dent in even the largest of projects. My clients are often surprised to find that they can accomplish something in one week that they had thought would take a month. Computer programmers call this a "sprint." It's a short period of time where they go all out to try to build something new. I find that thinking about your week in the same way leverages Parkinson's law to your maximal benefit.

No matter how big my goals are (writing and promoting this book took almost two years), I always break those goals into weekly sprints that I can cognitively manage. Thus I'm constantly leveraging Parkinson's law in my favor. Working like this generates a beneficial type of stress called eustress that keeps me primed and motivated. We'll talk more about eustress in Part 2 of this book.

CHAPTER RECAP

Killing yourself at work but still "losing the week" is no way to live. If you want to start hitting your goals without getting burned out or having to be perfect all the time, then you should zoom out to view your productivity with a more generous lens. I recommend playing your game on a weekly basis, because a week is a good-sized increment of time in which you can get a lot wrong and still pull out the win by Friday evening.

You'll find that a weekly approach forms the basis of a powerful feedback loop. It opens up infinite paths to winning your week, even as it's a far more humane way to live and work. A weekly approach will help you keep your perspective on what's really important and keep you on the right side of Parkinson's law. Most of all, it encourages you to synchronize all your productivity skills into a cohesive whole, leading to that breakthrough where your performance improves even as work starts to feel easier.

Hopefully I've convinced you, or at least gotten you interested. Let's start exploring The Winning The Week Method.

2

THE WINNING THE WEEK METHOD

WHICH WOULD YOU SAY IS MORE CRUCIAL TO WINNING YOUR week—planning for the week or executing that plan? Abe Lincoln was very opinionated on this point. He thought that preparation was worth twice as much as execution:

> *"Give me six hours to chop down a tree, and I will spend the first four sharpening the ax."*
>
> **—ABRAHAM LINCOLN,** former president of the United States

He wasn't alone in this conviction. The wisest thinkers in history have told us repeatedly that planning is the key to winning.

> *"If you fail to plan, you are planning to fail."*
>
> **—BENJAMIN FRANKLIN,** Founding Father, author, statesman, postmaster general, diplomat, and inventor

"The general who wins the battle makes many calculations in his temple before the battle is fought. The general who loses makes but few calculations beforehand."

—SUN TZU, famous Chinese military strategist, general, and author of The Art of War

"Plans are worthless. But planning is indispensable."

—DWIGHT D. EISENHOWER, five-star general and former president of the United States

"Luck is what happens when preparation meets opportunity."

—SENECA, Stoic philosopher, statesman, and orator

Please try to prepare yourself for what might be the least controversial statement anyone could make about productivity: planning your week ahead of time is the key to winning your week.

You might be saying "duh" right now. It certainly feels like an obvious statement. When I surveyed over five thousand professionals, asking them what it takes to win the week, 94 percent said that planning ahead was "key" to winning the week. So it sure seems like this is common knowledge, right? But when I followed up and asked those same five thousand people, "Have you conducted a planning session (ahead of time) for the past four weeks?" only 6 percent replied yes. After further defining what adequate planning looks like, that number dropped to less than 1 percent!

PLANNING YOUR WEEK AHEAD OF TIME IS THE KEY TO WINNING YOUR WEEK.

@DEMIRANDCAREY

So despite how obvious this statement seems, it's highly unusual to find someone who actually plans out their weeks on any consistent basis. There's a baffling gap between our beliefs and our behaviors when it comes to planning. How can we be aware that planning is key to winning, yet less than 1 percent of us are doing it?

A big part of it is mental. Planning sounds so neutral but is actually quite stress-inducing, forcing you to look at things you'd rather avoid. That generates resistance from the limbic system (also known as your "lizard brain"). This can cause a downward spiral so potent and self-sabotaging that I've devoted an entire chapter of this book to halting and reversing its effects (Chapter 3). For now, it's enough to say that most of us sabotage our planning before we even start.

It's also important to realize that most people don't know how to plan correctly. It's not something we are taught in school, the workplace, or anywhere else in life. Despite how critical good planning is to doing great work, we're left on our own to figure out how to do it. I'll show you that (since it's highly counterintuitive) most of us get it wrong and have predominantly negative experiences with planning. These planning "fails" further reinforce our negative associations with it.

Since planning goes directly against the grain of our nature, no one is born with it. Good planning is remarkably counterintuitive, because planning requires seeing your world clearly and being able to face the consequences of your actions. But in our "natural" state, we are motivated by fear, plagued by bias, and highly resistant to facing the consequences of our actions—all of which distorts or blocks our ability to see the world as it truly is, thus preventing us from planning successfully.

This happened to my client Anne. Unbeknownst to her, Anne was getting sabotaged by a cognitive bias called the Mere Urgency Effect. This describes our tendency as humans to prioritize urgent tasks over nonurgent ones—even when the nonurgent tasks have significantly higher payoffs. On its face, this makes no sense at all. We should be rational actors, carefully calculating the costs and benefits of our actions. But in reality, we're just emotional actors who have the ability—every once in a while—to act rationally.

Without a good planning process to counteract the Mere Urgency Effect, Anne was constantly getting sucked into urgent but unimportant work, at the expense of moving a crucial project forward. During a coaching session, she told me, "I feel like I'm taking crazy pills. Every week I tell myself that I'll get to the important work next week, but it's been over six months, and I haven't even opened the tab on my computer for [my most important project]. What is wrong with me?"

Even worse, researchers have found that this effect only gets stronger as we get busier. So Anne was stuck in a downward spiral caused by a cognitive bias, without even knowing it and without the tools to counteract it.

An excellent planning process was the tool she needed. Proper planning helps us to see the world as it really is, not distorted through the lens of our emotions and biases. This tool can help us walk through that minefield not just once, but consistently over long periods.

THE WINNING THE WEEK METHOD

Allow me to introduce The Winning The Week Method as that tool. Like the scientific method, it helps you move past your biases to see the world as it really is. It's a structured method for looking at your week and, in thirty minutes or less, gaming out all the relevant pathways to a win. It takes the form of a simple checklist designed to walk you through the most essential components of planning your week. But in practice, it's a methodology for consistently winning your weeks.

WHAT ABOUT MONTHLY AND ANNUAL PLANNING?

To keep this simple, I'm not going to discuss monthly and annual planning, though they are important. If you want to hear my take on those, check out **winningtheweek.com/resources**.

To achieve all of this in less than thirty minutes, a lot needs to happen underneath the surface. Let's review The Winning The Week Method at a high level. We'll be diving deep into each of these layers in the coming chapters.

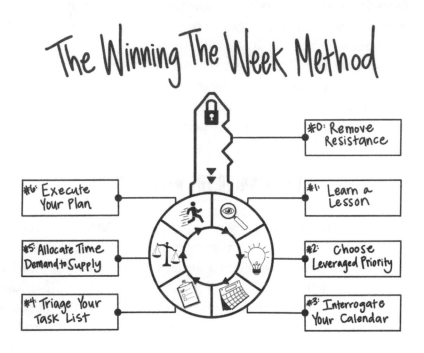

Download this image at **winningtheweek.com/resources**.

Step 0: Remove the Resistance

By adulthood, most of us carry around a deep resistance to the idea of planning our week. That's because planning one's week generates stress, anxiety, and fear—even under perfect conditions.

Anyone who has tried planning their week knows that it can be extremely anxiety-provoking. Like cleaning out your refrigerator and dreading what's inside of those containers, a good planning session forces you to face a week's worth of things you'd rather not look at. That kicks off a fight-or-flight response from your limbic brain—the part of your brain whose primary job is to move you away from pain and toward pleasure. This reaction to planning is a perfect example of how the limbic system can go haywire, perceiving something as a foe when it's really a friend.

That's why the first step of The Winning The Week Method is removing the deep, internal resistance almost all adults have to planning. The good news is that you can rewire your brain to not only tolerate a planning practice but even become highly addicted to it! We're going to talk about how to do that in Chapter 3.

Step 1: Learn a Lesson Each Week

Looking for a lesson or improvement each week is essential. This simple practice creates a positive feedback loop, wherein you get slightly better each week. Done correctly, this results in small but consistent improvements that compound readily and create a "snowball effect" within a few months. The impact is life-changing within one year. Your weekly sprints can become an opportunity to try new things, evaluate your wins and losses, and fine-tune your game.

Not for nothing, but this practice is also good for the soul. Our natural negativity bias compels us to focus on the negative—the things that didn't get done or the frustrations that haunt us. But even in a bad week, you usually get a lot of good work done! A simple five-minute review will make you feel good about all of the things you accomplished, countering your negativity bias. That's going to give you a much-needed psychological boost right as you get ready to plan your coming week.

Step 2: Choose a Leveraged Priority

Next, you decide on your priority for the coming week. Hands down, the biggest planning error is choosing the wrong priority (or choosing multiple priorities instead of one). This spreads your focus and dilutes your impact, trapping you in a vicious cycle of overwork where you begin falling behind on work and invariably try to make up for the shortfall by working longer hours. Eventually, you realize you're stuck in a cycle but have no idea how to escape.

In The Winning The Week Method, the focus is on effectiveness over efficiency, and nothing makes or breaks your effectiveness like your choice of priority. Done wrong, you run the risk of exhausting yourself and still being very unhappy with the outcome.

Step 3: Interrogate Your Calendar

Most folks think they know what a calendar represents, but they only see a small part of the picture. Your calendar isn't only for dentist appointments and meetings. It's a tool that can help you visualize and manage your entire supply of time—your precious 168 hours a week.

The problem is that people hate looking at their calendar, because it only shows them things they don't want to see. Filled with dread, most people will glance at their calendar only when absolutely necessary and then run away as fast as possible. But if you avoid your calendar, your time inventory isn't accurate, which plants the seeds for future disasters! These tiny errors are buried all over your calendar, like landmines waiting to explode.

Winning your week requires you to actively search out and expel these errors. To be able to truly trust your calendar, you'll have to interrogate it like a lawyer interrogating a witness. This goes far beyond the passive calendar "review" to reveal your true supply of time, often turning up hidden stores of time you didn't realize you had.

Step 4: Ruthlessly Triage Your Task List

The nature of human beings is to want to do more than they have time for. But in a world where you can't do it all, you need to ruthlessly triage your task list. That means letting go of the fantasy of "getting it all done" and asking a far better question: "How can I do the most good with my limited supply of time?"

In this step of The Winning The Week Method, you'll look at each task on your to-do list as a "bid" for your precious time. Knowing that not all bids can be accepted, you'll whittle down your to-do list to only consider the high-est-yielding bids for your time. This will take courage, because you're going to take flak no matter what you decide. Someone's request will have to lose out in order for the greatest good to be served. The only other option is unacceptable: trying (and failing) to make everyone happy and killing yourself in the process. We will provide you with crystal clear criteria for making these cuts, giving you the ability to justify your decisions to yourself and to the people around you.

Step 5: Allocate Time Demand to Supply

This is where you make the tough choices about what's really going to happen in your week, with eyes wide open to the consequences. Having interrogated your calendar and triaged your task list, you must now allocate demand to your fixed supply. In practice, that means allocating time in your calendar to get each task done (also known as "calendarizing" your task list).

This step is easy to understand but incredibly hard to do! This is where wishful thinking hits the hard wall of reality at full speed, which is why people avoid this step. But reconciling time supply and time demand is where the rubber meets the road; it's where you get traction and forward movement. The goal in this stage of The Winning The Week Method is to make the real choices so that your time supply equals your time demand. This is where your plan becomes a plan.

CHAPTER RECAP

The unavoidable fact is that you have to plan your week to win your week. Though most people intuitively know this, almost no one does it, in spite of our forefathers pointing to its importance for over a millennium.

The reason is that we're fundamentally emotional actors who have the ability (every once in a while) to act rationally. Once you accept that premise, you start to see how easy it is to fall victim to fear and bias. But just as the scientific method guides scientists past superstition and bias to create incredible breakthroughs, The Winning The Week Method will help you to see your world as it is, not distorted through the lens of fear and bias. It's a tool to help you walk across that minefield consistently over long periods to achieve incredible breakthroughs in your life. It doesn't come naturally, but anyone can do it with the right methodology. Cultivated over long periods of time, it can even begin to alter the way you think and become second nature.

Five simple elements are all you need for a fast and successful planning process:

1. Review your past week for lessons learned.
2. Get clarity on what's really important (versus what seems important) and decide on your one priority for the week.
3. Take an accurate inventory of your time supply.
4. Ruthlessly triage the demands (or bids) for your time.
5. Match time demand to time supply.

This list makes it seem so simple, doesn't it? Man, I wish it were that easy. I think you'll be surprised at how many hidden pitfalls you'll find once we start peeling this onion. Let's start with the biggest obstacle to winning your week that you will face: internal resistance to planning.

3

REMOVE THE RESISTANCE

I COULD TELL THAT GEORGE WAS QUICKLY BECOMING FURIOUS with me. He'd been trying to stay calm and explain himself, but his patience was wearing thin. He was getting red in the face, and I swear I saw some spittle fly past his camera.

George was attending an online master class I was teaching on The Winning The Week Method. I already knew George because this was the fourth time he had participated in my master class. He would stay through the question and answer session each time, challenging me on every part of the methodology. He seemed determined to prove to me that planning—at least for him—was impossible.

"Planning takes too much time!"

"Why create a plan if my boss is just going to blow it up?"

"My life is just too chaotic...planning doesn't work for me."

"I don't like how planning feels. It's too constricting!"

In my chat window, I got a private message from Carey:

> Why does this guy keep coming back if he's so sure that planning doesn't work for him?

I took a deep breath and interjected. "George, let's talk about the real reason why planning isn't working for you."

* * *

STEP 0: REMOVE THE RESISTANCE

It's humbling to say that I taught this method for many years and failed to reach at least half of my clients. I knew the methodology worked, but half of my clients would give up before they even got to the starting line. And I couldn't understand why.

Today I know what was missing. I call it Step 0 in The Winning The Week Method, because it's something that has to be done before we can begin: counteracting the deep, internal resistance nearly all adults have to planning. If you don't do this, you've lost before you've even started, and you'll never succeed in creating a planning practice.

The Winning The Week Method

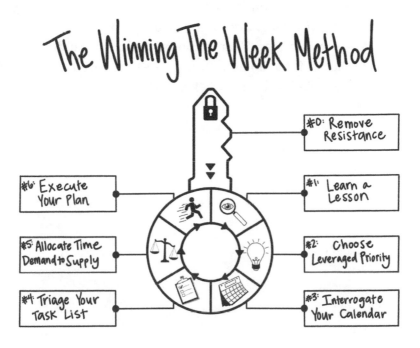

#0: Remove Resistance

#1: Learn a Lesson

#2: Choose Leveraged Priority

#3: Interrogate Your Calendar

#4: Triage Your Task List

#5: Allocate Time Demand to Supply

#6: Execute Your Plan

This resistance is so powerful because it originates deep within our brain, from a part of the brain that can override our logic. The limbic system (also called the "lizard brain") is the part of our brain controlling our behavioral and emotional responses (among other things). It's constantly on the lookout for threats to our safety; you could say that its primary job is to move us away from pain and toward pleasure.

The limbic system kicks off a fight-or-flight response when it perceives a threat to our life. But this is where things can get complicated. It's also why our hearts race when we're about to ask our boss for a raise. You see, any flavor of anxiety can trigger a fight-or-flight response. We know (logically) that there is no threat to our life when asking our boss for a raise. However, our limbic system still registers it as a potentially life-threatening situation. Clearly, this part of our brain hasn't kept up with the world we live in now. It mistakes some positive situations (like asking for a raise) as threats and mistakes some negative experiences (like smoking cigarettes or taking drugs) as desirable. Planning the week is a perfect example of how the limbic system can go haywire, perceiving something as a foe when it's really a friend.

If you've ever tried planning your week, you know that it can be extremely anxiety-provoking. Even in a perfect planning session, you will feel stress, anxiety, and fear. That actually means you're doing it right! Stop and take that in for a moment. It makes sense because a good planning session entails facing down a week's worth of fear and anxiety in one short session.

EVEN IN A PERFECT PLANNING SESSION, YOU WILL FEEL STRESS, ANXIETY, AND FEAR. THAT MEANS YOU'RE DOING IT RIGHT!

@DEMIRANDCAREY

That feeling is more than enough to fire your limbic system and (over time) plant the seeds of a negative association with planning in your brain, often a very potent and lasting association. By adulthood, almost all of us have developed some form of resistance to planning. For some unlucky people, just the idea of planning their week can generate a violent negative response.

That brings me back to George. Every time I disarmed one of George's objections, he would just bring up another. His lizard brain had already decided it wanted to avoid planning, and it hijacked his logic brain to generate a never-ending stream of rationalizations. That's why nothing was getting through to him: deep down, George didn't want to be persuaded. His lizard brain was in charge, and his logic brain was only along for the ride.

Over time, these rationalizations can solidify into a narrative, which is just a story we tell ourselves about who we are and how the world works. Often, these narratives aren't true, but isn't that entirely the point? Our narratives help us justify the status quo in a way that's palatable for us. This is what was happening with George. At forty-five years old, George had over two decades of negative experiences with planning. This was more than enough time to solidify his narrative that "planning might work for other people, but it doesn't work for me!"

I took a moment to coach him on this issue since it was such an important point to address. Here's what I said:

> George, let's talk about the real reason why planning isn't working for you. We all have contradictions built into our personality: a conflict between the things we say we value versus the real values that our actions and behaviors reveal. When we're not loyal to something we decided to do—like planning our week—we're still being loyal to something underneath that. A hidden value that's even more important to us and that we're prioritizing over the thing we say we want.

> I'm guessing that you keep coming back to this class because you can't resolve this conflict. I imagine you're attracted to this topic, George, because you see yourself as the kind of person who's on offense, not defense. And a part of you knows that planning your week is fundamental to getting on offense. I imagine that's an important stated value to you.

> But deep down, you also value safety. Feeling secure. And I'm just guessing here, but I imagine that looking at all the ways your week can go wrong makes you feel very unsafe and insecure. So your lizard brain and your logic brain are going to battle, and unfortunately, your lizard brain is winning out right now. You're valuing safety over getting on offense. Does that resonate?

For a second, George looked even angrier, and I thought I must have missed the mark. But then he said, "Jeez, am I really that transparent?"

Relieved, I went on.

> No man, you're not. Who here feels just like George...you just didn't want to say it?

Over a dozen hands went up.

> George, ironically, valuing safety above all else can lead you to some very unsafe places. You have to allow yourself to feel unsafe in some ways to become the person you want to be and operate the way you want to in life. Let me show you how to rewire this resistance to planning and even turn it into a craving.

* * *

I promise you this: if you have a deep resistance to the idea of planning your week, you're not alone! Maybe you badly want to start planning your week but just can't seem to bring yourself to do it. There's good news. You can rewire your brain to not only tolerate a planning practice but even become highly addicted to it! Let's talk about how to do that.

Weekly planning is a habit like any other. In Charles Duhigg's fantastic book *The Power of Habit*, he identifies three simple elements of a sustained habit: cue, routine, and reward. He calls this the "Habit Loop" because it happens again and again, ingraining itself deeper and deeper into our brain each time.

The cue is the stimulus that triggers the loop to begin, such as the sound of your phone dinging with an alert. The second the cue hits, your brain springs into action to perform the habit. Since this loop has been completed countless times, the cue puts the brain into a state of anticipation even before the reward is provided, like Pavlov's dog salivating at the sound of the bell.

The routine is the action you have to take to secure the reward. When performing a well-oiled habit, the brain enters a state of automaticity, where the next steps happen almost unconsciously and with minimal cognitive load. If you've ever "woken up" to realize that you've been driving a familiar route for an hour, you've experienced this automaticity. It's almost a zombie-like state.

The reward anchors everything into place. Without the reward, the loop would never form because the lizard brain only saves the loops that result in a positive and memorable reward. The evolutionary advantage of this simple mechanism is self-evident: it's a shortcut that makes it easier and more pleasurable to take actions that ensure your survival.

You should approach your planning habit just like building any other positive habit loop, and build in a reward. Unfortunately, people treat planning like a "necessary evil," forgetting that it needs to have some kind of reward attached to it—not because you "deserve" a reward, but because no habit loop can establish itself without a juicy reward. Otherwise, the lizard brain will quickly associate planning with anxiety and reject it outright.

If you're like most of my clients, you're probably not starting with a clean slate. Even if you badly want to create a planning habit, you likely already have a deep resistance built up to the thought of planning. Maybe you even have an intense revulsion to it. In either case, don't worry—you'll be surprised how quickly you can turn that around.

MY TRANSFORMATION FROM RESISTANCE TO CRAVING

I'll admit that even after planning weekly for years, I still had to do battle with myself when it came time to sit down and plan out the week. I was utterly convinced of its utility and even addicted to the long-term benefits. But like a patient gagging on their medicine, I still had intense resistance to sitting down and starting. All of that changed one sunny morning in Paris. The last of my resistance to planning my week finally became a craving that lasts to this day.

On a sunny Friday morning in Paris's 15th arrondissement, Carey and I packed up and left our rented apartment. We were in the midst of the "digital nomad" phase of our life, enjoying the fact that we could live and work from anywhere in the world. We were wrapping up a two-week stay in Paris, and it was our last day. Checkout time for our Airbnb was eleven in the morning, but our flight wasn't until eleven at night, so we had a lot of time to kill. Our usual game plan in this type of situation is to find a lovely little café where we can crack open our laptops and do some work. So I found a café with great reviews, and we zipped off in an Uber.

But we were not prepared for how cool this café was! Granted, every café in Paris is pretty cool. But this one put them all to shame, with a view of the Eiffel Tower, delightful music, and effortlessly fabulous French patrons in whose company we felt chic and sophisticated. We took a seat, opened our laptops, and since it was the end of the week, proceeded to plan out the coming week.

We must have spent a couple hours in that lovely café. It was a "Kodak moment." Even today, I can close my eyes and see that café in vivid detail. As we were leaving, Carey turned to me and said, "Do you know, at home, it's like pulling teeth to do our weekly planning. But this was so fun. I could do it like this for the rest of my life!" She hit the nail on the head.

That's when the lightbulb went on. Carey had just solved the biggest problem we never even knew we were facing with our planning. Even though we had been planning our week for years, we had never tried to make it fun. We never thought of making planning a reward in and of itself.

When we came back from Paris, we were on a mission to recreate that vibe at home. We found the fanciest café in our town—total French bistro vibe—and did our weekly planning there every Saturday morning. The waiters knew us by name and saved a booth just for us. And even though we finished our planning in just thirty minutes, we would stay for hours sometimes, connecting and talking. It was like date night for us, but better. We faced our fears about the coming week together and shared the relief that comes after a good planning session. Something about that relief made us feel more connected, and we found that those hours right after a planning session were ideal moments for us to catch up and talk. For years, we never missed a week.

I knew I was hooked on my planning habit when I stopped wanting to go out on Friday nights because I didn't want to miss out on those exquisite Saturday mornings! Those planning sessions had become the highlight of my week. Once we had a solid plan for the week in place, we could connect on a deeper level, laughing like we had when we first started dating.

RE-ARCHITECTING YOUR WEEKLY PLANNING SESSION

A good planning habit has a potent reward attached to it, but an unstoppable planning session is its own reward. So if you don't have a weekly planning session you love right now, I want you to consider scrapping it and starting over.

Here are some of the ways people have created a planning session that's rewarding in and of itself:

- My client Caleb and his wife meet at a wine bar on Friday nights after work. They plan their week over a bottle of their favorite Beaujolais, then take the rest of the time to relax and connect.
- Emma has a husband who doesn't like planning, so she wakes up early on Saturday to do it herself. She bakes two frozen chocolate croissants from Trader Joe's—one to eat at the start of the session and one when she finishes. Not only does she get a great planning session in before anyone wakes up, but she also gets crucial personal time—which isn't easy as a mother of five!
- Many of my clients have copied our Saturday morning "French café" idea at a local café, complete with frothy lattes and croissants. It's luxurious and affordable for most folks, and it's an easy time to get childcare.
- Gene goes to a Russian bathhouse in Manhattan every Saturday around lunchtime. After a quick soak in the hot tub, he has lunch and pre-plans his week. Then he closes his laptop and spends a couple hours listening to podcasts in a sauna, sweating out the stress of the week.

A GOOD PLANNING HABIT HAS A
POTENT REWARD ATTACHED TO IT, BUT
AN UNSTOPPABLE PLANNING HABIT IS A
REWARD IN AND OF ITSELF.

@DEMIRANDCAREY

DO YOU REALLY NEED TO MAKE PLANNING FUN AND REWARDING?

I've seen many clients fail at this step by thinking that they can keep their planning sessions dry and dull and give themselves a pathetic reward at the end. My client Wes tried to force himself to sit down at the kitchen table and plan his week, with the promise that he could have one square of dark chocolate afterward. His lizard brain wasn't fooled, and he didn't get his planning habit off the ground (until he scrapped it and created a juicier planning experience).

I recommend you do your weekly planning somewhere incredibly fun and upbeat, or at least in a safe space. These environments generate serotonin, oxytocin, and other reward chemicals, which means that just being there is a reward in and of itself. You should also reward yourself again once the planning session is complete, to reinforce the positive association. Carey and I always high-five each other at the end of our planning session and say, "Good job!" That might sound like a thin reward, but we both crave each other's approval, so on top of the luxurious café experience, it feels significant. Plus, who doesn't love a great high-five?

FOCUS ON THE BENEFITS OF PLANNING TO OVERCOME RESISTANCE

Even after transforming your planning session into something intrinsically rewarding, you can keep building positive sentiment around planning. One critical mental hack is to focus on the rewards that planning provides in the short, medium, and long term. And that's easy because there are so many! It's impossible to do a weekly planning session and not reap extraordinary benefits.

Your lizard brain is fabulous at sniffing out things that benefit you. It will quickly connect the dots between the short-term benefits. With time, it will also register the medium- and long-term benefits, solidifying a positive relationship with planning. Eventually, you'll realize that you aren't just rationally drawn to planning; you're emotionally drawn to it! You're hooked on it (in a good way).

Here are some examples of short-term rewards you can expect right away:

- Linda remembered during her planning session that she had a huge deliverable due first thing on Monday. Imagine walking into the office and realizing that! Having discovered it on Friday, she had time to prepare for it.
- Stephen discovered that he had agreed to a meeting but had forgotten to put it on his calendar. Oops! Crisis averted.
- Basma realized her daughters had an "away game" for field hockey that she had volunteered to drive for. If that had snuck up on her, it could have been disastrous.

In the medium term, here are the kinds of payoffs you can expect to see:
- After four weeks of consistent weekly planning, Erich felt "caught up" for the first time in years.
- Wendi liberated time one day a week to create better systems for her business, immediately offloading work that had been weighing her down.
- Jeremy finally got the chance to create a meal plan, an essential move for a single father.

But the most potent rewards come in the long term:
- Anne (from the prior chapter) was able to counteract the Mere Urgency Effect and finally see herself moving the ball forward powerfully each month. And other people started noticing, ultimately resulting in a significant new career opportunity.
- Despite working as a top manager at Microsoft, Amita started making time to take her kids to South Asian cultural events, eventually volunteering for a prominent role at her temple.
- Over the course of a year, Moshe turned his side hustle into a full-time business, fulfilling a lifelong dream.

CHAPTER RECAP

The reason that less than 1 percent of people regularly plan their week is simple: most people have unconsciously built a resistance to planning over time. That makes sense because planning is inherently stressful! The most powerful thing you can do to overcome this resistance to planning is to transform it into a powerful craving. And the simplest way to do that is to design a weekly planning session that is a powerful reward in and of itself.

Focus your attention on the pleasure of the environment you have chosen, the powerful release that comes after your session, and whatever reward you choose to cap off your planning. You'll find it's less challenging to motivate yourself to sit down and plan your week. As the rewards from planning keep flowing in, you'll quickly become addicted to planning when your lizard brain connects the dots and decides that it is undeniably a good thing. Your job is to prove to your lizard brain that planning is working powerfully and giving you what you value: freedom, power, control, completion, and satisfaction.

It's not easy to create a new habit, and planning is no exception. But I encourage you to connect to the intrinsic values you see yourself having, like being a person of integrity, someone who faces their difficulties instead of running away, and someone who is on offense, not defense. Decide right now: How will you address the resistance that you have to planning? How can you redesign your environment to start craving your planning sessions instead of avoiding them? What's your version of that café in Paris?

Believe it or not, this was the hardest part. Now that you're past this barrier, I will show you how to turn your weekly planning into a feedback loop and massively accelerate your progress in the process.

4

LEARN A LESSON
EACH WEEK

"The best way to change long-term behavior is with short-term feedback."

—SETH GODIN

MY HIGH SCHOOL SOCCER TEAM WAS THE WORST IN OUR LEAGUE. We even got clobbered by the other terrible teams in the league.

In my sophomore year, the senior members of the team were sick of it. They got everyone together at the start of the season and made them swear an oath to place at the top of the league. Don't get your hopes up; we didn't even get close. In fact, it was our worst year ever. I remember one of our lowest points was a game in nearby Modesto, California. It was late in the season, and it was clear that we were going to rank even worse than the previous year. The mood was already sour when we took to the field but got rapidly worse as we took a thorough beating from the other team. As they expertly picked us apart, our best striker couldn't handle the indignity anymore. Frustrated, he started playing dirty, hurting other players, and trying (unsuccessfully) to employ harassment and intimidation. He rightly got a red card. Even though we had more games left in the season, I never saw him at practice again. He was so frustrated that he never came back, not even to quit. The following year, he joined the football team.

You're probably thinking we didn't care if we were bad or not, but that's not true. We desperately wanted to be good—or at least not so terrible! But I now realize there was a defect built into the way our team practiced that would never allow us to win: we didn't have a feedback loop in place. A winning soccer team would go back the next day and rewatch the recording of the game to identify what went wrong and what went right. From those learnings, they would decide what to focus on in the next practice. Each game would provide new and essential information to their feedback loop, regardless of whether they won or lost. The feedback loop of a winning soccer team is *practice, play, rewatch, practice, play, rewatch.*

Without a feedback loop, we lacked awareness of our weak spots, which would have been obvious if we had taken a moment to rewatch our games. So we kept repeating the same mistakes, and our best intentions couldn't override this defect built into our team structure. I call this phenomenon "stepping on the rake" because it reminds me of a clown show at the circus. The clown steps on a garden rake, and the handle smacks him right in the face. He looks dazed and confused, but then he steps on it again! The audience is laughing and yelling at him to stop, but he does it again...and again. There's pathos in that humor, because we've all done this in some area of our lives—unwittingly making the same mistakes over and over for lack of awareness. We feel like a fool in the process, but we don't really know how to escape the cycle.

The same thing can happen with your productivity game. Even if you intend to improve, you'll constantly get clobbered if you don't have a feedback loop in place. It can be so frustrating that it makes you want to quit. Blind repetition is the enemy of progress because it gobbles up all of your energy without moving you forward. If you examine your own experience, you'll see that simple repetition is not enough. My soccer team practiced hard, but we didn't practice smart.

STEP 1: LEARN A LESSON EACH WEEK

What my team needed was intentional, deliberate practice. Psychologist Anders Ericsson coined the term "deliberate practice" while researching how people become experts in their fields. Deliberate practice differs from regular practice in its relentless focus on being purposeful and systematic in getting better. It aims to minimize wasted effort in order to improve as rapidly as possible. Ericsson admits that this is easier said than done. To maintain deliberate practice, he notes, you have to fight a strongly ingrained tendency to fall into autopilot, where you stop paying attention and miss opportunities for improvement.

The key to bringing deliberate practice into your productivity game is having an effective feedback loop that gives you honest, unvarnished feedback, meaning feedback that lets you know if you're getting better, staying the same, or getting worse.

In his book, Ericsson shares a story of Benjamin Franklin. Having been told by his father that he was a poor writer, Franklin desperately wanted to learn to write beautifully and persuasively. He designed the following program of improvement:

> [Franklin] began to study his favorite articles from a popular British publication, *The Spectator*. Days after he'd read an article he particularly enjoyed, he would try to reconstruct it from memory in his own words. Then he would compare it with the original, so he could discover and correct his faults. He also worked to improve his sense of language by translating the articles into rhyming verse and then from verse back into prose.

Now pause for a moment and think about your game—the work that you want to take to the highest possible level. Have you approached it with the same level of seriousness that Franklin did? Have you built feedback loops into your process? If not, why isn't your development every bit as important to you as Franklin's was to him?

I've got exciting news for you. You can add many of the benefits of deliberate practice to your productivity game with just five minutes of focused reflection added to your weekly planning session. This forms the foundation of a feedback loop: reflecting constructively on your performance from the past week and finding one deliberate way to improve your game.

My client Chitra shared a great example of how this worked for her:

> Funny story. I added five minutes of reflection to my weekly planning over a month ago. From those reflections I realized that everything that has gone wrong in my life in the past month resulted from saying "yes" to something I should have said "no" to. I already knew I was a people-pleaser, but I never saw just how badly it hurt my progress. After a month of seeing my self-sabotage in action, I finally see that connection clearly. This week I practiced saying "no" and had the best week I've had in a long time!

Another client, Aaron, shared how his feedback loop led to a counterintuitive realization:

> It's been about two months since I started the reflection practice. I wish I could say it was an instant success, but that first month was really rough. I set what I thought were small goals, but I still couldn't hit them. But I realized that was a huge learning by itself because it made me step back and ask, "Why don't I have the time to accomplish even these small goals?" That led me to change my focus to reducing work and simplifying rather than trying to push through even more work. My big learning was that I have to do less today to create a foundation to do more tomorrow.

BETTER QUESTIONS YIELD BETTER ANSWERS

Self-reflection done poorly traps you in a maze where you're lost in endless navel-gazing. I've developed two questions to help you get you quick, valuable insights.

The first is what I call the Groundhog Day Question. I love the movie *Groundhog Day*, with Bill Murray. The protagonist, Phil, becomes trapped in a time loop, reliving the same day repeatedly. He can't change outside forces (like the storm that traps him in that small town), but he can perfect his actions and reactions to those circumstances. Eventually, Phil arrives at a Nirvana-like state. He achieves the perfect execution of his day inside the time loop, learning how to be a better human being in the process.

What if you could relive the past week over and over again, and discover what "perfect" looks like for you? You wouldn't be able to change your outside circumstances, like last-minute interruptions and emergencies, but you could change your approach and your reactions. I find this thought exercise incredibly useful, putting you in exactly the right mindset to learn fantastic lessons from the past week. Think about the following question:

If you could relive the past week a thousand times, what would the perfect execution have looked like?

This question is powerful because it completely changes your frame of reference. Instead of focusing on negative feelings about your performance (guilt, shame, and regret), it brings your focus to how you could have managed yourself better. This question is incredibly entertaining because it allows you to replay the game in your mind and fantasize about how to optimize your performance.

The lessons you learn from this exercise are highly applicable to your future! Like my soccer team in high school, if you can't see where you went wrong, the chances are high that you will keep making the same mistakes that you did in the past. Earlier I called this phenomenon "stepping on the rake," comparing these mistakes to a clown stepping on a garden rake again and again. When you genuinely see where you went wrong and what you should have done differently, you're removing the rake so you never step on it again.

Here are a couple more examples to stimulate your thinking:

- Chitra realized that she was saying "yes" too reflexively, ambushing her productivity in the process.
- Aaron learned that he was loading himself with too much busywork, preventing himself from making even the smallest amount of progress on his bigger priorities.
- Lukas saw that his days were chopped up by meetings, to the point where the remaining hours weren't usable for getting good work done.
- Kendra saw that she wasn't scheduling enough time between appointments, which meant she was always running scared!
- Lachlan discovered that he only planned work events (not personal events), so fun things never happened in his free time.

THE DOUBLE DOWN QUESTION

Another blind spot in our self-reflection comes from our negativity bias. This is another cognitive bias (that we all share) where we tend to notice what's wrong more than what's right and dwell on the negative. All of that focus on the negative means we often overlook the positive. In the process, we often stop doing something that was working, for lack of recognizing its positive impact. In other words, we are biased toward seeing what's wrong and forget to continue doing what's *right*. You know this has happened to you if you've ever said, "Gosh, that thing was working so well. Why did I ever stop doing it?" There's an easy way to counter that, with what I call the Double Down Question.

Ask yourself, "What worked well this week that I should double down on next week?"

News flash: the easiest way to improve is to figure out what's already working and just do more of that! Here are a few of my favorite examples of clients noticing something good and doing more of it.

My client Sherie, an ophthalmologist from New Jersey, said:

Normally, I wake up tired every day. It feels like a huge chore just getting up and ready for the day. By the time my brain "gets in gear," I'm already seeing patients and taking meetings. Then the day is over, and I veg out for the rest of the night, usually staying up too late.

But last month, I got jet-lagged from a long trip and fell asleep an hour earlier every night, and VOILA! I felt so much better in the mornings! I know it's so obvious, but I guess I was totally under-slept and needed that extra hour of sleep. So this month, I just kept that early bedtime going, and I've been feeling way more energetic and alert.

Pretty simple, right? She saw something was working and just kept it going! Another client of mine, Tim, runs a law firm in California.

This week I got mad at my team for asking me small-ball questions all the time. That anger motivated me to create a standard operating procedure that I probably should have created years ago. It only took me a couple hours in the end, but it's already saved me that much time this week. I heard your voice in my head saying, "Okay, that worked. What if you kept doing this?" So I blocked off two hours every Friday morning just to iron out these small processes that frustrate me.

(Post-script: one year later, Tim has been running his law firm remotely from his beach house, with his toes in the sand.)

CHAPTER RECAP

Your weekly pre-planning session is a golden opportunity to create a positive feedback loop, where you can invite deliberate practice into your game and massively accelerate yourself toward mastery. Improvements can be made in leaps and bounds when you choose just one small thing to do better each week.

This is the first practical step in your weekly planning session. You'll take five minutes to reflect on your past week and try to find one powerful lesson, then use that to improve your performance in the coming week. This simple step forms the foundation of a powerful feedback loop in your productivity game. At the very least, you'll see where you can stop stepping on the rake, making fewer unforced errors. But you can accomplish so much more: this is a chance to experiment with your productivity game and evaluate the outcomes, which will result in small but consistent improvements that build upon each other exponentially.

The hardest part of this process is setting your ego aside and genuinely stretching to see around your cognitive blockages. You'll need to apply genuine curiosity to unearth the best learnings. Using the Groundhog Day and Double Down questions will help you do that. For more resources and a downloadable cheat sheet, go to **winningtheweek.com/resources**.

In the next step, we'll tackle one of the most vexing issues in productivity: deciding on your priority for the week.

5

CHOOSE A LEVERAGED PRIORITY

YOU'RE PROBABLY ALREADY SEEING THAT THIS PRODUCTIVITY GAME is counterintuitive, which can lead to moments of extreme frustration. As a result, I get some very "passionate" (meaning angry) messages from clients. I got this one via Facebook Messenger:

> Hey, Coach Demir. I'm really struggling with you telling me I can only choose one priority each week.
>
> Some background on me: I'm a wife, mother of three, and project manager coordinating over fifty people. I'm used to spinning twelve plates, but things are spinning out of control. I got forced into a title-only promotion at work, which means three times the work with no additional pay. On top of that, my daughter is suddenly struggling socially and academically. And my son expects me to be his personal chauffeur for his baseball aspirations. If that wasn't enough, I play

a crucial financial role in keeping my local church afloat. All of this means that my husband and I barely get a chance to speak if it's not about getting things done, and I'm afraid of the toll it's taking on our marriage.

So when you tell me to choose just one priority above all others—with my life—I'm sorry, but it makes me feel crazy! I feel like either you are criminally negligent for saying that (just kidding) or I'm missing something super important. I just don't know how I could ever choose one priority when I have twenty things that are all so important! Can you help?

—Mandy

I nodded as I read this because I have been there myself, and I remember the feeling well! We've all been there, haven't we? Mandy is going crazy because she has no effective filter for what comes first and what comes next. Everything is her top priority in her world, and being asked to choose one over the other made her feel like a parent being asked to choose between children.

But she also knows that, by definition, she cannot have more than one priority at a time, just like there cannot be more than one gold medal winner at the Olympics. The moment that first place is shared, it is not first place anymore. Garr Reynolds summed it up perfectly:

> If everything is important, then nothing is important. If everything is a priority, then nothing is a priority.

It's easy to get painted into this corner and feel completely helpless, like Mandy. My promise is that by the end of this chapter, you'll have a framework that will always reveal your most important priority—no matter how busy you are.

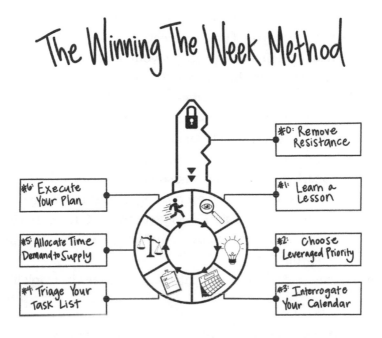

The Winning The Week Method

#0: Remove Resistance

#1: Learn a Lesson

#2: Choose Leveraged Priority

#3: Interrogate Your Calendar

#4: Triage Your Task List

#5: Allocate Time Demand to Supply

#6: Execute Your Plan

STEP 2: CHOOSE YOUR LEVERAGED PRIORITY

Step 2 of The Winning The Week Method is to set your primary goal for the week. Your priority is the thing—over all other things—that must be accomplished.

Let's clear something up before we go on: your priority is not the *only* thing you'll do this week. Quite the opposite—it's probably just one of a thousand things you'll do! Rather, your priority is the thing, above all others, that must be done. It's the task that must be put at the front of the line and given the right-of-way. Simply put, if you only accomplish that one thing, this week could *still* be considered a success. But if you fail to do it, this week will be a loss, no matter how many other tasks you accomplish.

Most people would agree with this. Where people trip up is in *choosing* that priority. Not choosing a priority, or selecting the wrong one, is easily the biggest mistake I see my clients making. And that's because, intuitively, most people choose their priority by asking themselves, "What is most important at this moment?"

That question feels so right, but it couldn't be more wrong. It is hands down the worst filter you could use for selecting your priority for this coming week. Let's run an experiment. Try asking yourself that question right now: "What is most important at this moment?" I promise you won't get just one thing popping into your mind—you'll get no less than five things, each one feeling more important than the last. Like a vague Google search, this question will bring you too many results and leave you overwhelmed.

If it wasn't already clear to you, life isn't a fair fight. Life can come at you from all directions, but you can only take on one thing at a time! If you try to do everything you want to do (and everything that is asked of you) through conventional means, you will lose. Life is just too big. But like David battling Goliath, you can win an unfair fight by identifying a key advantage and leveraging it to amplify your force.

If we naturally use a bad filter, what would a better filter look like?

NEW CRITERIA FOR PICKING THE RIGHT PRIORITY

Enter Gary Keller and Jay Papasan, authors of *The One Thing*. They offer a simple but counterintuitive framework for choosing your top priority. Instead of asking, "What feels most important right now?" they ask:

> What is the one thing you can do such that, by doing it, everything else becomes easier or unnecessary?

Keller and Papasan make an ironclad case that we should be more focused on making the accomplishment of future tasks easier instead of simply getting as many tasks done today as possible. They argue that each task on your list appears manageable in isolation. But when you start adding them together, they quickly become unmanageable. Each additional task costs time, costs energy, and incurs "switching costs" (which is the time and energy it takes to switch between tasks). That means that the cost curve of additional tasks is much steeper than we might have believed. So instead of prioritizing what *feels* important, the filter should focus on what makes your life and work consistently *easier*.

I admit this one was a head-scratcher for me at first—mainly because (at that point in my life) I didn't believe that things could actually become easier, especially as my goals became bigger and bolder. All of my experience up to that point had taught me that life just gets harder and harder. If you can shed that false narrative, this new filter will make complete sense. Best of all, it actually works!

Imagine a delivery person tasked with delivering groceries to a home. With just one delivery to make, she simply grabs the bags, and off she goes.

But if you task her with delivering ten homes' worth of grocery bags, she will have a dilemma. You could tell her to "prioritize" the deliveries, but that's not going to help much. There are simply too many bags to hold! Working faster (or harder) is not a solution to this problem. No amount of "hard work" or "grit" is going to fit forty grocery bags on this poor person's arms. There's just too much to handle! Sound familiar?

What would really solve this delivery person's problem would be something that made the job itself easier—like a cart.

As the scale of the problem grows, the delivery person should be stepping back on a regular basis to look at the bigger picture, exploring tools or methods to help get the job done at scale. Ironically, we humans tend to do the opposite. The bigger the sense of overwhelm, the more we dig in to our existing tactics. So her answer to "what feels most important right now?" will always be working harder and faster, not building a cart. Yet, according to Keller and Papasan, building a cart is exactly what she should be doing.

BRINGING LEVERAGE TO YOUR GOAL SETTING

I will call this new type of priority your "leveraged priority."

The classic definition of a lever is something that amplifies an input force to provide a greater output force. You've probably heard that ants can lift up to five thousand times their own body weight; this is because they have hard exoskeletons and highly engineered joints, which form levers that amplify their lifting ability. Human muscles don't work that way. But with a basic understanding of physics, we can use a shovel to pry a rock from the ground, demonstrating the same principle. Leveraging your actions applies this powerful concept to your productivity, amplifying your force tenfold. That means you can do more with less input.

Let's combine these concepts of force amplification and Keller and Papasan's Leveraging Question to select your priority for the week. Your leveraged priority for the week is the action that amplifies your force today *and* makes future tasks easier.

YOUR LEVERAGED PRIORITY FOR THE WEEK IS THE ACTION THAT AMPLIFIES YOUR FORCE TODAY AND MAKES FUTURE TASKS EASIER.

@DEMIRANDCAREY

I cannot emphasize how crucial this concept is to winning your week. By choosing a leveraged priority, you will expend less energy, even as you accomplish much more than you thought possible, and life will seem to get easier over time. Without leverage, it's just a matter of time before the overwhelm overtakes you.

HOW IT WORKS IN THE REAL WORLD

Remember my client Mandy, from the beginning of this chapter? Let's see how this new way of thinking changed her perspective in our next coaching session.

"Listen, Mandy," I said. "I get where you're coming from. You're totally overwhelmed, and right now, you feel like the only answer is to somehow find more hours to get it all done. So let's pull that thread. What's something that would create some extra time for you, not just this week, but every week for the rest of the year? I think we can both agree that this would be highly leveraged for you right now."

"I'm drawing a blank," she replied. "I swear there's nothing like that!"

Mandy's mind went blank, which is something that can happen when our fight-or-flight response has been triggered. In that mode we can't see anything but the problem. We lose perspective and have a hard time coming up with solutions. I tried an exercise, which I love, to help her move out of her limbic brain and into creative thinking.

"Let's take five minutes and make a list of twenty things that could create extra time for you. No idea is bad. Just give me everything you can think of."

Her twelfth idea hit on something interesting.

"Well," she said, "I'm basically a part-time chauffeur, driving my kids to their activities in the afternoons. If I didn't have to do that, I would probably get back ten hours a week. But I can't possibly afford a private driver!"

"That's a great idea," I said. "Let's not give up on it just yet. What would you do if you got sent to the hospital for a month? How would your kids get to their practice in that scenario?"

We brainstormed that question for a few minutes until the lightbulb went on for Mandy.

"Actually, I have a nephew who has his driver's license," she said. "Maybe I could ask him to stay at school and do his homework, then drive my kids home after practice. He'd basically be getting paid to do his homework, but it would be a lot more affordable than a private driver."

Fast-forward one month and Mandy had hired her nephew and saved the ten hours a week that she expected. But more importantly, she realized how draining all that driving had been on her energy. All that energy came flooding back, and she used it to tackle her other challenges with newfound gusto.

When we checked back in, I could tell she was happy but was also dealing with some cognitive dissonance:

"It's just hard to wrap my mind around. In retrospect, getting someone to drive the kids was so obvious. But I wasn't even thinking about it! It just makes me wonder how many other leverage points there might be in my life, hiding in plain sight?"

I nodded my head. I said, "That's the weirdest thing about leverage. We don't think about leverage naturally; we just think about getting it all done. Strangely, the most leveraged action for most of my clients isn't even on their to-do list. You need to step away from the front lines of your life and get some perspective to find it."

"That's so true!" Mandy replied. "Like one of those 3D posters from the nineties. You have to just keep staring at it until the image pops out."

Here are some other examples of leveraged priorities to help you brainstorm your own leverage points:

- Implementing a new system for your team that could save you sixty hours over the next year
- Turning a new presentation into a reusable template so that all future presentations are easier and faster to make
- Implementing a chore system at home to save everyone time and take the load off of an overworked spouse
- Identifying and firing the bottom 5 percent of your clients who suck up most of your time and energy, freeing you to find better clients who pay you more and take up less time
- Writing this book is highly leveraged for us (Carey and me). It moves our mission forward and helps us reach more people. But it also increases our trust and credibility, making it easier for us

to reach new audiences. That helps our online ad conversions and gets us invited to speak on podcasts and news networks.

Take five minutes at this point in your pre-planning to choose a highly leveraged yet attainable goal for the week. If you aren't sure if something is leveraged, ask yourself the Leveraging Question:

What action can I take that makes everything else easier or unnecessary?

CHAPTER RECAP

At the beginning of this chapter, I said that choosing the right priority is the number one thing that most people are messing up. They fall into the trap of selecting a priority by asking themselves, "What feels like the most important thing right now?" That question will lead them into Mandy's dilemma; they will be overwhelmed by all the things they have to do and unable to choose among them.

I introduced you to a much more powerful filter: the Leveraging Question. That filter will reveal the actions that amplify your efforts far beyond what you believed was possible. By utilizing the Leveraging Question, you will accomplish tasks that *both* are important *and* make your life permanently easier.

Whatever you do, don't skip this step! Remember that life is a massive opponent, making this a completely unfair fight. If you try to meet life head-on, you will lose. As David did when he fought Goliath, you need to choose your tactics wisely, find your most advantageous angle of attack, and then go all in. If you'd like to read more examples of leveraged priorities, go to **winningtheweek.com/resources**.

Once you've found your leveraged goal, it's time to clear the path to attain that goal. This is where your ambition meets cold, hard reality.

6

INTERROGATE YOUR CALENDAR

"The man who has anticipated the coming of troubles takes away their power when they arrive."

—SENECA

MY CLIENT AGI HAD "ONE OF THOSE" WEEKS—THE KIND WHERE things start going wrong on Monday and just keep getting worse. It was a pivotal week for Agi at work, with a crucial moment where she needed to "bring home the bacon" at her job. But life decided to throw some surprises her way.

First, her nanny called in sick for the entire week, and it couldn't have been a worse week to be alone with the kids. On Tuesday, Agi's daughter forgot to tell her she needed a ride to a volleyball tournament. On Wednesday, her boss (who had previously said he loved her presentation) changed his mind and asked her to scratch it and start again—the day before the meeting! Then, on her way to the critical meeting on Thursday, she hit freak traffic caused by a major accident. Finally, on Friday, her boss asked her to deliver all of the materials they promised to the client by Monday morning, meaning she would have to work nonstop over the weekend.

Have you ever had a week like this, where things start going sideways, and they just don't stop? Sometimes it's a pileup of different issues, like Agi's week, and sometimes it's one big mistake that ricochets through your week like shrapnel. Often the best response you can muster is to simply try to survive it.

I think we've all had weeks like this. In this chapter, I'll show you a crucial technique to prevent this from happening—or at least make it a lot less frequent.

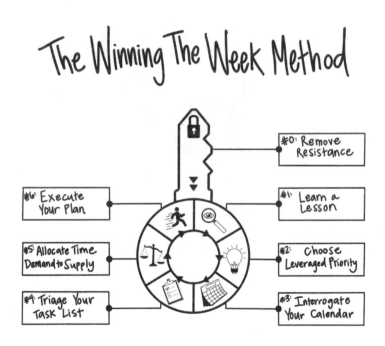

STEP 3: INTERROGATE YOUR CALENDAR

Most folks think they know what a calendar represents, but they're only seeing a small part of the picture. Your calendar isn't *only* for reminding you about dentist appointments and team meetings. It represents something far more valuable: your limited supply of time.

You only have 168 hours each week. Once you subtract sleeping hours, commute time, personal care, family responsibilities, and so on, you end up with about sixty hours with which to conduct the business of your life. This picture becomes even grimmer when you match that time against your *energy*. We've all experienced the feeling of having *time* to work on something in the evening but being so tired that you don't have the *energy* to do it. In my experience, people only have about four hours a day at peak energy, which means that we only have about twenty hours a week to do our very best work. That's not a lot!

There's stiff competition for your scarce time. Not only do you have a lot to accomplish for yourself; other people want you to do things too. And they can be very persuasive! This hard fact—that there are a tiny number of productive hours and stiff competition for those hours—means there will never be enough time to go around. Someone will always be disappointed in the way you spend your time. You will be too.

I like comparing time supply to truffles (the mushroom, not the chocolate). The problem with truffles is they can't be easily cultivated. Even with insatiable demand for truffles, suppliers can't make many more of them, just as we can't make more time. That means the price is sky-high—one small Italian white truffle can retail for $211! Truffles have another thing in common with time: they have a short shelf life. A truffle starts losing its signature odor in just five days. Because they are so valuable, so supply-constrained, and so perishable, there's an entire industry built up around carefully taking inventory, harvesting, shipping, and storing truffles.

Your time is also a nonrenewable resource. You can't create, buy, or rent any more of it. And it won't store well. It's highly perishable, and once it's gone, it's gone forever. That means you have to defend it fiercely and allocate it with great care.

Truffle sellers treat their truffles like diamonds, because failure to carefully track your truffle supply could result in disasters like
- Selling product you didn't have in stock
- Allowing product to go bad on the shelves
- Having product stolen from you without your knowledge

- Leaving money on the table by not getting the best price for your limited supply

Similarly, your life is your business, and your time is the inventory in that business. You can sell your time to others, consume it yourself, or it can go bad. As such, you need to keep an accurate inventory of the time you have available versus time that's already claimed. Failure to do so results in some of the most common productivity errors:

- Overcommitting with time you don't have
- Not effectively using the time you do have
- Having your time "stolen" from you by other people
- Not allocating your time to the most impactful work

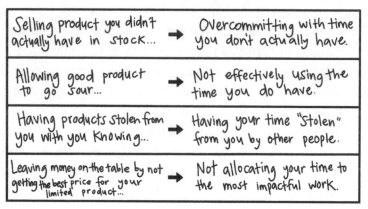

YOUR TIME IS YOUR INVENTORY

Selling product you didn't actually have in stock... ➡	Overcommitting with time you don't actually have.
Allowing good product to go sour... ➡	Not effectively using the time you do have.
Having products stolen from you with you knowing... ➡	Having your time "stolen" from you by other people.
Leaving money on the table by not getting the best price for your limited product... ➡	Not allocating your time to the most impactful work.

This is why I hate it when people call this step in planning a calendar "review." Review makes it sound painless, like checking movie times online. Taking an inventory of a precious resource is serious business!

The problem is that, in practice, people hate looking at their calendar. They think it only shows them things they don't want to see: the places they have to be, the things they have to do, and the people they have to meet—all of which they don't want to do. That negative association means that most people will glance at their calendar only when absolutely necessary, then run away as fast as possible.

This poor maintenance of your time inventory plants the seeds of disasters waiting to happen: that tennis tournament you forgot that you signed up to drive your kids to or the meeting that got changed from 9:00 a.m. to 12:00 p.m. and now conflicts with another appointment. These minor errors are buried all over your calendar, like landmines waiting to explode.

In this chapter, I will show you how to quickly inventory your time supply to make the most of this precious resource and prevent yourself from ever having a week like Agi's ever again.

THE HIT-AND-RUN CALENDAR REVIEW

The biggest problem with the traditional calendar review is that most people are doing what I call a "hit-and-run" calendar review. This is what Agi was doing. She was opening her calendar, briefly glancing at it, and then running away like the cops were chasing her. Sadly, you don't make problems go away by ignoring them, so these innocuous problems festered and grew until they exploded at the worst possible time for Agi.

I call these problems "landmines" because they are buried all over your calendar, waiting to explode in your week. Think back to Agi's nightmare week that I described at the beginning of this chapter. Her kids' volleyball game was always there, lurking in the background. She just didn't remember it until it blew up in her face. And she knew her boss was probably going to ask her for last-minute changes and quick turnarounds—because he frequently did. These issues could have been anticipated if Agi had searched them out.

In fact, right now, a situation is forming that will blow up in your face— you just don't know about it yet. If you can discover it ahead of time, you can diffuse it safely. If you don't, you'll step on that landmine and it will explode. The shrapnel of that landmine won't just blow up your day; it could damage the rest of your week and even affect the lives of people around you. When these things explode, they explode big time, causing massive collateral damage.

In this step of The Winning The Week Method, your job is to find these landmines and deactivate them in advance. I call this "interrogating your calendar." Like a lawyer seeking the truth from a reluctant witness, your calendar isn't just going to show you the information you're seeking. You have to sweat the information out of it! You have to be clever and come at it from all angles, questioning the information you get and validating that it's true.

HOW TO INTERROGATE YOUR CALENDAR

Here's a process we've created to make this fast and relatively painless. Take a few minutes to open up your calendar and review the next *fourteen days*. I realize that sounds strange because most people will just look at the next seven days. But that forms a blind spot in your plan. If you only review Sunday to Sunday, what happens if you have a big project due the following Monday? That project would be lurking in your blind spot, showing up when it's too late. You should review the next fourteen days, every seven days, creating a rolling overlap that prevents any sneaky landmines from lurking in your blind spots.

Here are some helpful questions to ask as you interrogate your calendar:

1. What Shouldn't Be on Your Calendar?

Many of my clients have events on their calendars that they don't plan to attend. These can include unnecessary meetings, social events, recurring reminder appointments, and many more. When I ask them why they keep these calendar invites, they typically say, "I guess I didn't bother to delete it."

Decline and erase these events so they don't clutter your calendar. Make sure every event on your calendar is something you absolutely will attend.

2. What Should Be on Your Calendar but Isn't?

Don't allow anything to be assumed or taken for granted. If it's a "hard-edged" commitment (meaning you have to be at a specific place at a particular time—even via teleconference), then make sure that you block off *all of the time* it will take.

For example, let's say that you have a meeting this Thursday. At first glance, it looks like a one-hour Zoom meeting. But upon closer inspection, you realize that it's in-person at the office. At that hour of the day, it'll take you an hour to get there and an hour back. But if you're honest, you also need to add fifteen minutes on either side to transition to the car and get going. So this one-hour meeting actually takes three and a half hours in your calendar. Now imagine that a coworker had seen that you were free right after that meeting and booked you for another meeting (that you couldn't possibly attend since you'll be driving back). This is a classic example of a landmine: small mistakes compounding on each other to become a big problem.

As you can imagine, this is a common error that gets people into trouble by luring them into thinking they have more time and space than they actually do. Here are some other examples of things that should be in your calendar but usually aren't:

- Preparation time for important meetings
- Travel time to and from events
- Meetings you committed to but never scheduled
- Time needed to transition between different types of work
- Recurring events that you stop putting in your calendar because you figure you'll remember them

Take the time now to scrutinize your calendar for things that *should* be there but aren't.

3. How Much "Flex Time" Will You Need to Deal with Emergencies This Week?

There are always things that will pop up without warning, and if you're smart, you'll set aside time to deal with those preemptively. It's usually last-minute emergencies that pull you off your number one priority but still have to get done because they are highly urgent. I call this type of unknown work "UUW," which stands for "unplanned, unwanted work." In the story about my client Agi, her UUW arose when her boss asked her to redo her entire presentation the day before the crucial meeting. She was angry that she had to do that, but when I asked her if she was surprised, she said, "Not really... my boss always makes requests like that." So it was something she could have reasonably set aside time for, but didn't. That's her bad in my book.

UUWs happen to all of us in one way or another, so the intelligent move is to preemptively block off chunks of time in your calendar to deal with unforeseen issues that are bound to come up. I label those blocks of time "UUW" in my calendar, and I think of this as flex time built into my week. I don't know *when* I'll need that time, but I know that I *will*! Building in this flex time is a powerful way to plan for the unexpected and provide much-needed lubrication to keep the gears of your life from grinding you to bits.

Is it worthwhile to block off time when you have no idea how much time you'll need? Sure it is. In the scenario where you *underestimate* how much time you'll need next week, you'll still thank your past self for every extra minute you bought yourself. And if you *overestimate* how much time you need, you can work ahead on your task list—no harm done. You can always find productive ways to use flex time if you don't need it. But you can't create that extra time if you have already stuffed your calendar with commitments.

I suggest you start by giving yourself one hour of UUW time for each working day of the week (five hours a week for most people). Then scale it up or down depending on whether it feels like enough. Where possible, I recommend placing those UUW time blocks toward the end of the day and the end of the week because work tends to pile up in those spots. Visit **winningtheweek.com/resources** for a supplemental training on UUWs.

Before we move on, stop and take a moment to look at your calendar. Block off as much UUW time as you can spare, starting with five hours for the week.

4. What Could Be Arranged More Optimally in Your Calendar?

Pre-planning is your chance to dictate how you'll spend your time this week, so why not make it as convenient and streamlined as possible? For example, if you need to do several chores around town, why not do them all on the same day instead of scattering them throughout your week?

The principle at work here is *consolidation*: allowing yourself to get into a mode of action and stay in that mode. Consolidation reduces your cognitive load because doing the same types of things takes less mental energy than constantly switching between different activities. It works. You'll find that you can get far more accomplished and not feel exhausted at the end of the day. I can tell you with great certainty that days with high levels of consolidation are highly productive and give you an intense sensation of forward momentum. And you're not as tired at the end of them.

Here are some of examples of what consolidation looks like for some of my clients:

- Consolidating all meetings on certain days to maximize focused work blocks
- Doing one big shop and meal prep session over the weekend, instead of a little bit every night
- Saving up household tasks and chores for one day per month, allowing you to gear up into "chore mode" (on my chore day, I preemptively pull out all my tools to be completely ready for the long list of chores I'll be taking on)
- Scheduling a planning session with your kids to discuss the events for the coming week and what they need, instead of them constantly interrupting you with requests throughout the week

As soon as you start looking for opportunities to consolidate your calendar, you'll see them everywhere!

5. When (Exactly) Will Your Leveraged Priority Get Done?

Go ahead and estimate the amount of time it will take to get your number one priority done this week. Then add some buffer to that estimate. Now schedule that time directly into your calendar, ideally on Monday or Tuesday (when your energy and attention are at their peak).

Suppose you find that (even after optimizing your calendar) you don't have enough available time to complete your leveraged priority. In that case, it's time to adjust that goal to something else that's achievable within the limitations of your week. Or go back and renegotiate your other responsibilities more aggressively. Remember to look for leverage—the things you can do to make life easier or more efficient down the line.

6. Where Are the Landmines in My Calendar?

Ask yourself, "What landmines will explode in my week?" Your job is to find them and deactivate them in advance. They could be anywhere. I recommend you take a "mental walk" through every part of every day in your coming week, asking yourself where the landmines might be hiding. Slowly and methodically investigate every time block in your calendar. Look out for anything that could catch you off guard, like a family member's birthday, an anniversary, an important meeting, or tricky travel logistics that could leave you troubleshooting on the fly.

In all likelihood, the landmines will come from predictable sources, such as your kids, your family, your boss, or a demanding client. Think back to the landmines that have exploded in the last four weeks. The causes of those are the most likely sources of future landmines, because even if history does not exactly repeat itself, it sure will resemble itself.

For each landmine, decide on a plan to diffuse that situation before it happens. If there's nothing you can do in advance, write out a response plan to reduce the pain of that landmine exploding. I recommend you save your landmines in a list, because that list will become your customized trigger list for catching landmines in the future. This trigger list will make it easier and easier over time for you to identify and diffuse the landmines that you repeatedly encounter in your life.

7. Did My Calendar Review Unearth Some Hidden Tasks?

If you're doing this correctly, you will think of new tasks and uncover hidden tasks as you're interrogating your calendar. Try not to get sucked in to dealing with them. Just write them down and save them on the side. We'll be tackling those in the next step.

GOING PRO: TAKING A GREAT CALENDAR INTERROGATION AND

MAKING IT EXCEPTIONAL

Asking these simple questions will make your calendar game stronger than almost everyone's out there. But you can take it even further. To take your planning to the highest level, ask yourself what is *likely* to go wrong and figure out how to head that off before it happens.

The Stoics called this concept *premeditatio malorum ("the* premeditation of future evils"), an exercise in imagining all the things that could go wrong or be taken away from us. In the Lifehack Method, we frequently call this "wargaming your week." War games are used in military strategy to simulate a battle before the first shot is fired. The purpose of a war game is to play out all possible scenarios, thus preparing oneself for any eventuality. It's *premeditatio malorum* applied to war. It's a powerful exercise that has been taken up by leaders of all disciplines. Once you're familiar with the concept, you begin to see that it's already being employed all around you:

- Soccer coaches wargame their strategy for the upcoming game against a formidable opponent. They ask themselves how the other team might respond to various offensive strategies and how they would respond in kind.
- CEOs wargame their competition, asking themselves how competitors might try to steal market share or respond to their new products.
- Hedge fund managers wargame their portfolio performance, asking themselves which investments might lose value if the jobs report coming out the next week is unfavorable.

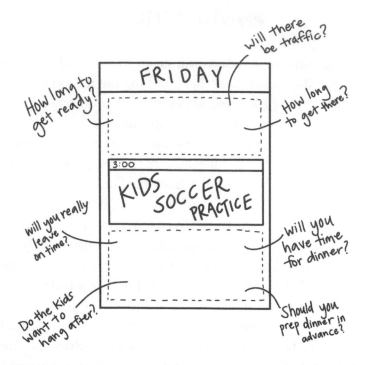

The point of the exercise isn't just to morbidly think about what bad things could happen to you this coming week. It's to find the vulnerabilities in your plan and fix them before they take you out. The idea is to be prepared for anything so that you aren't negatively surprised and taken off guard when the unexpected occurs. This allows you to set events in motion to head off the worst outcomes and brings the focus to the things you can actually control.

AGI, REVISITED

I asked Agi to revisit her nightmare week and replay it in her mind, using the principles we talked about in this chapter. Here's what she found:

I knew my nanny was sick when she left on Friday. It wasn't impossible to think that she might not come in to work on Monday; I just didn't want to consider that possibility. And my daughter's game was an unforced error: I just didn't put it on the calendar. Same thing with the traffic: I should have given myself twice as much time to get there, knowing how important that meeting was. The fact that I didn't was an oversight. If I had really interrogated my calendar, I would have found four or five easy-to-avoid landmines.

My boss is trickier. I didn't know he would ask for a rewrite, but he's done it before. A lot, actually. Same with setting unrealistic deadlines to deliver clients materials. Overpromising is sort of his MO (to make himself look good to our clients). If I had wargamed my week, I might have caught one or both of those and been able to anticipate it. In fact, this past week I saw a meeting where I thought he might over-promise what our team can do. So I brought it up to him and reminded him that we're overcommitted and under-resourced, and could he please not add anything to our plate in that meeting? He laughed and sort of brushed it off. But in the meeting, he didn't overcommit. I call that a win!

CHAPTER RECAP

Time is your most limited resource, representing the supply side of your productivity equation. Most people avoid facing this fact because they don't want to see how limited their time is. But that is precisely what hamstrings your success. The Winning The Week Method takes the opposite approach—you step into radical ownership of your time by taking a thorough time inventory. Ironically, by treating time as precious and limited, you'll create more time abundance and freedom than you ever thought possible.

In practice, this happens during a well-conducted interrogation of your calendar. In this chapter, I showed you how to do a proper calendar interrogation, eliminating landmines and creating a reliable model of your time supply. I also showed you how to take it to another level: wargaming your week. You learned to cast your mind into all the possible ways your win could be stolen from you, a critical step to preventing that from happening. As Sun Tzu said, "Every battle is won before it is fought." By identifying every potential landmine and removing its power over you, you've set yourself up to win the week before you check in to work on Monday morning. Download a cheat sheet for interrogating your calendar at **winningtheweek.com/resources**.

Now it's time to look at the opposite side of the ledger from time supply—your time demands.

7

TRIAGE YOUR TASK LIST

"You can do anything, but not everything."

—DAVID ALLEN

AT THE START OF THE NAPOLEONIC WARS IN 1803, THE HORRID BATTLE conditions caused as many as one-third of the French troops to die in combat or from illness. This surge of deaths prompted a considerable innovation in medicine, led by military doctor Dominique-Jean Larrey. With so many injured soldiers coming in for treatment at once, doctors attempted to save everyone and ended up overwhelmed. Larrey recognized that trying to save every life was actually resulting in more deaths overall, as doctors ineffectively allocated their time to attempting to save every soldier.

To save more lives, Larrey developed the modern system of triage, which is still used today in hospitals and battlefields around the world. Triage is a classification system for assigning degrees of urgency to wounds and ultimately informs the order of treatment. Soldiers were categorized into three groups: dangerously wounded, less dangerously wounded, and slightly wounded. Instead of treating patients in the order they came in, doctors treated them using this triage system. The primary goal was to preserve the lives of the soldiers who would be able to fight again on the battlefield, and the secondary goal was to save those who had the best chance of recovery.

These doctors had to make the hardest call imaginable: treat every person equally (knowing more would die overall) or knowingly allow some to die (so that more could live). The triage system empowered those doctors—sworn to save lives—to make that difficult call. Importantly, this gave them treatment criteria that they could justify ethically to themselves and the world.

This is precisely what you need in your productivity battle. Whenever I'm looking at my lengthy to-do list, I put myself in the shoes of one of those Napoleonic military doctors. My tasks are my patients, all begging for my skills and time to help them. And I'm the doctor, deciding how to triage those tasks so that I can *do the most good with my fixed resources*. As much as I might want to, I know I can't get all these tasks done. I need criteria similar to the triage system so that I can justify these tough choices to myself and the people around me.

In its simplest form, here are my criteria:

- First, I want to accomplish my number one leveraged priority because that creates the most value for everyone and makes my life easier over time.
- Second, I want to tackle my other essential tasks in a way that balances urgency with impact.

My client Agi (from the last chapter) was shocked when I explained this to her.

"But Demir, I have to get everything on my list done. My boss is demanding that I do it all."

"Okay," I said. "Then tell me, when was the last time you got your whole task list done by the end of the week?"

She sighed. "Touché. Come to think about it, I don't think I've ever actually completed my whole to-do list. But it still feels like something I'm expected to do."

As human beings we want to do more things than we have time for. It's our nature! Agi can't get everything on her list done for one simple reason: there will always be more to do than she has time for. If she magically discovered ten hours of free time, I promise you, within a few weeks she would fill up that time with new ambitious responsibilities. So let's accept that creating more time isn't the answer, because we would just take on more responsibilities.

In a world where you can't do it all, you need to triage. You need to decide, with confidence, which tasks should get done and which ones should get pushed off. Rest assured, you're going to take flak no matter what you decide, because someone will always be unhappy with the call you make. So how are you going to justify your decisions when people interrogate you about them?

If you're reading this book, you're probably a knowledge worker, which means you're a professional who creates value using your brain rather than your hands. The greatest attribute of a knowledge worker is the ability to triage tasks to create the most value within fixed time and resources. To do that, you have to make tough choices and balance resources against competing priorities. Put more brutally, you have to get comfortable letting some patients die to maximize the good you can do overall. Knowledge workers are not paid to be "yes" people (even though it sure can seem like they are). We're paid to make tough decisions about what gets done and what doesn't get done to maximize the greatest good.

THE NATURE OF HUMAN BEINGS IS TO WANT TO DO MORE THINGS THAN THEY HAVE TIME FOR.

@DEMIRANDCAREY

What would your boss prefer—that you hit your big performance goals for the year or answer every email within twenty minutes? They'd like you to do both, but if they had to choose (and they do), they'd take hitting the big goals every time. Similarly, what would your clients prefer—that you make yourself available to them 24/7 or that you give a service that provides them with 10x value? Again, they'd like both, but in a world where they can't have both, they'll take the latter. Winning the week means choosing to get the *right* things done at the expense of getting *everything* done.

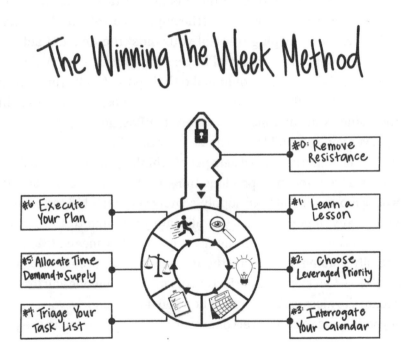

STEP 4: TRIAGE YOUR TASK LIST

In Step 4 of The Winning The Week Method, you will ruthlessly triage the tasks on your list, using a filter I will provide you.

In this step, you're scrubbing your to-do list and reviewing all of your commitments for the coming week to make sure you have an accurate picture of the demands on your time. If your calendar represents your time *supply*, your to-do list reveals your time *demand*.

Most folks think they know what a task list represents, but again, they only see part of the picture. Your to-do list isn't just for storing tasks. It's a tool that captures (and reflects back to you) the *demands* on your time. It shows you all of the things you want to do with your time, as well as the things other people would like you to do for them. And since your time is a fixed resource, the demand for time always outstrips the supply.

In my earlier example of a truffle business, I talked about the importance of keeping accurate inventory (the supply side of your business). But equally important is keeping track of your bids (the demand side of your business), represented as potential buyers for your truffles. A clever seller of a finite good like a truffle would make their potential buyers bid against each other so the seller can get the best price possible for their limited inventory. Since you can't make any more truffles, getting the best price is the only lever you can pull to maximize your benefit.

I like this example because it gets people thinking about each task on their to-do list as a "bid" for their precious time. In the business of your life, you always have more demand than supply, so not everyone's bid can be accepted, making it vitally important that you allocate your time to the highest and best use (in other words, to do the most good). That means tracking these bids carefully, valuing them correctly, and making them compete against one another. Even when executed perfectly, this means someone will lose out, but you'll create the most value overall. When you do this poorly, you sacrifice the greater good trying to serve everyone, overwhelming yourself in the process.

The problem is that people hate looking at their to-do list even more than they hate looking at their calendar. Looking at the mountain of demands on their time (and sensing how little time they have) would make anyone feel dejected and stressed. The resulting dread means that most people avoid opening their to-do lists. When they do, they gravitate toward the easiest, least overwhelming tasks while ignoring the rest. In my truffle example, that would be like selling your whole harvest to the first buyer without searching for better offers or comparing bids.

Worse, as you neglect your to-do list and the demands on your time become overgrown, the result is a pileup of backlogged tasks. The longer that list becomes, the more critical it is that you face it but, ironically, the more your internal resistance to facing it grows. This is the "avoidance death spiral." Most people opt for the easy way out—just doing the tasks that are blowing up in front of their face. That's fine for playing defense, but this strategy will never get you on offense. You can't consistently win the week that way.

WHY DOES CALENDAR INTERROGATION COME FIRST?

I frequently get asked, "Why do we start with time supply and then go to time demand? Can I triage my to-do list before I interrogate my calendar?" I recommend interrogating your calendar first, then moving to triage your to-do list because your time supply is fixed. Since your time is the primary constraint, it's better to get a sense of how much of it you have (or don't have) before thinking about what you want to accomplish this week. Otherwise, you'll get your heart set on a goal that you don't have the time to complete.

TASK TRIAGE IN PRACTICE

An excellent triage session means whittling down your to-do list so that you're only considering the highest-yielding bids for your time.

The first step is to hold on to that radical clarity you created earlier. Break down your leveraged priority into its supporting subtasks and add them to your to-do list. I can't tell you how many of my clients leave their most important tasks off their to-do list entirely, possibly thinking, "This is so important, I definitely won't forget about it." But of course, they do forget about it! So take your priority and break it down into all of its subtasks (even those that other people have to do). Make sure those crucial tasks don't get buried beneath less important—but more urgent—tasks.

Next, scan your projects and ongoing responsibilities and think about the tasks you need to do to keep them moving forward. To help my clients remember anything they might overlook, I have them create a list of possible places tasks might be hiding.

Finally, offload any nagging tasks. David Allen, the author of *Getting Things Done*, calls this "closing your open loops" because these tasks are the things your brain keeps looping on. I call them "brain flies" because they're constantly buzzing around your head and keeping you from concentrating—like remembering that you need to clean out the garage or schedule a dentist appointment. Looping on these tasks is a waste of energy and attention. Allen recommends banishing these energy-sucking tasks from your brain with a mental spring cleaning that he calls a "brain dump." And he's right—you need to swat those flies so you can concentrate on the important stuff. But there's also a trap here that I want to put some caution tape around. The tasks need to leave your brain, but most of them shouldn't go into your to-do list.

The majority of these brain flies are "Someday Tasks," meaning that you want to do them someday, but they aren't crucial to do this week. Or even this month. What most people do in a brain dump is load all of this crap into their to-do list. But cramming your to-do list with Someday Tasks is a recipe for failure because your list quickly becomes too overwhelming to look at, which causes something I call "task overload."

Imagine pushing a wheelbarrow full of gravel. The more gravel you add in, the heavier the wheelbarrow becomes, and the more energy required to push it. It's the same with your task list. The more tasks you dump onto your list, the more energy you have to expend mentally to process that list. Tasks like "clean out the hallway closet" or "learn Swedish" don't belong on your list until they become your leveraged priority or incredibly urgent. Here are some real-world examples of Someday Tasks volunteered by my clients:

- "We should build a dashboard to have our data in one place."
- "We should evaluate this outsourced CFO company."
- "We should create an exit survey for departing clients."

Notice the word "should" being used a lot here. That's a dead giveaway that it's a Someday Task.

There is a way to get the best of both worlds, getting these out of your brain without clogging up your task list. Create a separate list from your to-do list and call it your "Someday List." When you conduct a brain dump, throw it all in there, and then only move tasks from that list to your to-do list based on the Live-or-Die Task Triage Process that I'll show you below. My Someday List is a simple Google Document. You could also use a Word doc, a spreadsheet, or a list inside your task management platform.

Once a month, I review my Someday List to see if anything has gained urgency or importance. If it has, I move that task to my to-do list. In this way, your Someday List serves as a kind of limbo for bids on your time. You get the satisfaction of getting these brain flies out of your head and putting them somewhere safe, but they don't clog up your primary to-do list and create that sense of overwhelm that we all know too well.

Before we move past the Someday List, let me say one more thing: the majority of your Someday Tasks will hang out on that list until they're not relevant anymore and you end up deleting them. That might be a painful thought, but remember the idea of triage. You can't accept every bid for your time, so the next best thing is to choose the best bids and maximize the good you can do with the limited time you have. Get comfortable with the idea that something can be completely worthy of your time, but you still might not ever get around to it. That concept requires real maturity to embrace.

GET COMFORTABLE WITH THE IDEA THAT
SOMETHING CAN BE COMPLETELY WORTHY
OF YOUR TIME, BUT YOU STILL MIGHT NOT
EVER GET AROUND TO IT.

@DEMIRANDCAREY

Once you're done putting tasks on your Someday List, you still probably have a giant to-do list. Let me show you my criteria for how to tackle it.

WHERE TO STORE YOUR TASKS

Where you store your tasks is important. I've seen clients use sticky notes, their phone, their email, and a piece of paper—all at the same time. Instead of storing tasks on multiple lists, in various formats, you should stick to one list, in one place. Ideally, this list is created digitally, using a task management tool like Asana, ClickUp, or monday.com. My team uses Asana so that we can include all the documents, instructions, and links we'll need to complete each task in one place. For more on task storage, go to winningtheweek.com/resources.

THE LIVE-OR-DIE TASK TRIAGE PROCESS

Ruthlessly triaging your task list in only a few minutes would be impossible for most people. That's why I created this decision tree to help you decide if a task should get done this week, has to wait, or should die altogether.

1. Is It Related to Your Number One Leveraged Weekly Priority?
✓ If yes, it should stay on your to-do list! Brainstorm all possible subtasks and dependencies, including tasks that other people have to do.

➡ If no, move on to the next question.

2. Is It Incredibly Time-Sensitive?

I love this quote from Dwight D. Eisenhower: "I have two kinds of problems, the urgent and the important. The urgent are not important, and the important are never urgent."

This statement is true in theory, but in practice, you likely have tasks that have to get done if you don't want to risk getting fired or losing business. I promise that when you start tackling your work with leverage, you'll start seeing fewer and fewer of these urgent/unimportant tasks pop up. But for now, as long as you've already put your key priority first, you can also keep urgent tasks on your list.

✓ If yes, keep it on your task list. Ask yourself what has to be sacrificed to make room for this urgent but unimportant task.

⮕ If no, move on to the next question.

3. Can This Task Be TACO'd?

Invariably, you'll find that you have more tasks than anyone could do, even if they worked around the clock. I have a fun acronym, TACO, that can help you cut down the size of your to-do list as you're processing it. It stands for Terminate, Automate, Consolidate, and Outsource. Ask yourself the following questions:

Does this task truly need to be done, or can it be Terminated?

You'll be shocked at how many tasks you'll find on your lists that are either already complete or don't need to happen at all. Delete those tasks from your list. I understand how absurd this can sound. My client Rahul laughed when I suggested that he could terminate tasks altogether. But after ten minutes of brainstorming, he suddenly came up with a great example:

"Well, I've been the PTA president at my kid's school for four years in a row. Maybe it's time to let someone else take the reins. I spend hundreds of hours a year in that role!"

Later that day, Rahul took thirty minutes to write a polite resignation email and freed up hundreds of hours in one fell swoop. That was an epic example of "terminate."

Can this task be Automated? Can I make this task faster using technology?

Sometimes we overlook the fact that there could be a way to do all or part of a task using software instead of doing it ourselves. There are so many new programs that make things easier to do these days. One of my favorites is Zapier, which helps two otherwise separate softwares speak to each other. In my case, it automatically creates a new row in a Google Sheet whenever someone books a meeting with me using my scheduling link. This way, my team can easily calculate the total appointments booked that month, by whom, and for what purpose.

So ask yourself, "Is there a technology you can use to automate all or part of a task?"

Can this task be Consolidated? Could I achieve better efficiency by doing this task alongside similar work at the same time?

Consolidation means grouping similar tasks together on your calendar so that you can optimize your brain energy. The more task-switching you do, the less productive you are, so this strategy can dramatically boost your productivity. If you see an opportunity for consolidation, go ahead and group those tasks together on your list.

Another example of consolidation is calls and meetings. If you're already spending most of your day in calls and meetings, it's efficient to go ahead and schedule more calls and meetings for that day. Let's be honest, you weren't going to get great work done on that day anyway, so why not pull more meetings into that day and get them done?

Can this task be Outsourced? Could this task be delegated to someone else?

Ask yourself, "What would need to happen to move this task to another person?" Maybe you'd need to write a set of instructions or provide a decision tree to explain how to accomplish a task. Or (my favorite) you could film a video or a screencast showing someone exactly how you do it correctly, then send that to them as a set of instructions.

✓ If you can terminate, automate, consolidate, or outsource the task, go ahead and do so now.

➡ If not, move on to the next question.

4. Is It a Someday Task?

If this task doesn't have a specific due date in the next month, it's likely a Someday Task. You know it's a Someday Task if it's not related to your key priority, there are no specific timelines attached to it, and no consequences result from not doing it this week (other than you being disappointed). These tasks muddy up the water and make it harder to see the crucial tasks—so get them off your list!

✓ If it's a Someday Task, move it off your to-do list and onto your Someday List.

➡️ If not, move on to the next question.

5. Do You Need More Information about the Task to Make It Actionable?

If the task has made it this far without being classified, it might require additional information. There may be things that you need to clarify, or you may need to have someone explain its priority relative to other projects.

Let's say your boss has asked you to help sell an important new client. But, as you think about this task, you realize that you need more clarity to execute it. For example, what deliverables does your boss want to see? A pitch deck, a well-crafted email, or simply your attendance at a meeting? What is the timeline for this task? Also, should this task be done before or after other seemingly time-sensitive tasks? Without understanding this, it's hard to triage appropriately.

Remember, it's okay to send it back and ask for more information!

✓ If you realize you need more clarity, kick it back to the sender and ask for more information.

HOW TO SAY NO TO REQUESTS FOR YOUR TIME DIPLOMATICALLY

Some of the reasons we overload ourselves are people-pleasing and wishful thinking. We don't want to disappoint the people around us! We can't help it—this is part of how humans evolved to be social creatures.

Saying no might damage our connection with another person, and we are hardwired to want to strengthen connections instead of weakening them. That's why it feels impossible to say no to some people's requests. For example, we often feel like we "can't" say no to our boss because they could get us fired, thereby jeopardizing our livelihood.

That's why the real trick of saying no is doing it in such a way that you strengthen that connection instead of damaging it, while maintaining your boundaries in the process. And yes, there are diplomatic ways to say no without hurting someone else's feelings and even increase your social status in the process.

Here's how to do it:

1. Don't Lead with "No"

Let's say your boss approaches you about adding another project to your task list.

Boss: "Hey there! Exciting news. We're moving forward with the Hartman deal, and I'd like you to run point on it. I'll need the pitch deck ready by Friday!"

You: "Wow, that's awesome. Very exciting. I'm honored that you want me to lead this project. Let me grab my task list, and I'll meet you in your office to discuss."

Notice how you didn't say yes or no to the new project. You said you're honored and excited and want to discuss it further. Next, transition to phase 2.

2. Place the Request in the Context of Existing Commitments and Responsibilities

Most unrealistic requests come from people who have lost sight of existing commitments they already agreed to take on (or committed you to). This is the moment to refresh their memory.

You: "I have my existing list of priorities right here. I'll need to bump one of these three big projects off my list for this week to take on the Hartman deal. Which one would you say needs to go so that Hartman can become my top priority?"

Notice how this puts the ball in your boss's court. Now it's up to them to figure out how to rebalance your workload and make it a win-win.

Boss: "You don't get it. This is a critical time for us. We need to get it all done."

You: "I understand. But the most important thing I can do is give you accurate tactical information so you can make strategic decisions. If I said we could get this all done, I'd be lying. That might feel good now, but it would put you in an impossible situation in the near future. This happened last quarter with the Reese account, remember? We took on too many big projects and couldn't get it across the finish line. So I'm not saying no to the Hartman project. I'm just letting you know something has to give if we're going to take it on in excellence."

You've responded admirably to their request. You didn't directly say no, but instead nested the discussion inside the larger issue of your capacity and existing commitments. And you reframed your resistance as an issue of integrity (i.e., not wanting to lie or give inaccurate information) instead of laziness or lack of team spirit.

This dialogue is based on an actual conversation my client Evan had with his boss. He told me he was terrified the entire time and that his boss left the meeting deeply unhappy (which left Evan wondering if he needed to update his résumé). But later that week, his department suddenly got approval to increase their headcount after a yearlong hiring freeze. Although his boss never said it, Evan strongly suspected it was due to drawing that boundary.

For more examples of saying no diplomatically, download my How To Say No cheat sheet at winningtheweek.com/resources.

CHAPTER RECAP

In this chapter, I compared your tasks to patients who need your care, and invited you to adopt a triage approach to your task list. As Napoleon Bonaparte's doctors discovered the hard way, trying to help everyone can backfire, resulting in more harm overall. The same happens when you try to attend to every task coming at you. It takes courage to make the tough decisions that will hurt someone directly today but serve the greater good in the long run. To do the most good, you need to acknowledge that your resources are limited, and make those tough tradeoffs with eyes wide open.

I showed you a decision tree to make this process a lot less painful, helping you quickly triage your tasks and justify those decisions to the people impacted by it. The result is a clear, short, and high-impact to-do list. Every time you put your tasks through this filter, the result will be a list that only contains the highest-yielding bids for your time—in other words, *a winning to-do list*. You can download the Live-or-Die Task Triage Process cheat sheet at **winningtheweek.com/resources**.

Now only one step remains: bringing it all together and solidifying your plan for a winning week.

8

ALLOCATE TIME DEMAND TO SUPPLY

EARLIER IN THE BOOK, I SHARED MY STORY ABOUT NEARLY DYING FROM overwork. And I told you that my doctor ordered me to go from working more than eighty hours a week to less than forty hours a week immediately. But I didn't tell you what happened next.

I walked out of my doctor's office in denial. I couldn't go home. Needing to think, I walked into Central Park. It was a chilly November day, and the cold, damp weather reflected my thoughts.

How can they expect me to cut my working hours in half—in one week? It's impossible!

I can definitely kiss my bonus goodbye!

I can't tell my boss...he'll think I can't handle the pressure, and I'll never get that promotion.

I guess I can say goodbye to having any sort of career. Or wealth. Jeez—what am I going to tell Carey?

It was getting dark, so I started the long subway ride home to Brooklyn, unsure what I would say to Carey. Somewhere on that hour-long train ride home, I began to get angry. Really angry. Not at the doctors, or myself, or anyone in particular. Just at the situation. The more I thought about it, the more indignant I felt. *Screw this! This is outrageous! I'm not going to go down like this.*

By the time I got off at my stop, I was red hot with outrage. I stalked into my house with purpose and sat down at the table. I opened my laptop, and with rare clarity, *I had the first real planning session of my life.* I call it the "first" because I had always been doing it half-heartedly before. I never wanted to make tough choices and face the reality of my situation. Some part of me was always resisting, holding back, or engaging in wishful thinking.

But my red-hot anger melted away that resistance. For once I had no fear. I finally had a compelling reason to choose what would get done and what wouldn't get done. Because of that, I didn't shy away from the tough choices. I started firing off emails, ruthlessly canceling appointments, and begging out of meetings. Instead of looking at my overgrown to-do list, I started a completely fresh list, only bringing over the "do-or-die" tasks.

Then I did something I had never thought to do before. I placed every intended task into my calendar, filling it up to the forty-hour mark. If I wanted to get eighty hours of work done in just forty hours, I knew I needed to designate on my calendar where and when each thing was going to get done. This was a jigsaw puzzle where every piece had to go in just so. I had to be precise in allocating my time.

This story would be so much better if I could tell you that it worked perfectly that first try—but of course, it didn't. Crucial tasks still didn't fit into my schedule, and I knew it wasn't a winning plan. But in my anger I refused to give up, so I doubled back to the beginning. I got clearer and more leveraged with my priority. I renegotiated timelines and found some tasks to automate. I cut away slivers of time from every project, asking myself, "What does *good enough* look like here?" It was slow, and it was painful. But before I went to bed that night, I had a plan to get everything done in forty hours—without getting fired. I followed that plan throughout that next week like my life depended on it. I studied my calendar like the Talmud, treating it like the very word of God. And it worked. I finished my work in 40.2 hours that next week.

For years afterwards, I couldn't explain what I was doing or why it worked. Today I know what I was doing right: I had stumbled upon the steps of The Winning The Week Method. Many of the steps I already knew but hadn't *embraced.* But the last step—putting every single task into my calendar—was something entirely new to me.

THE IMPORTANCE OF CALENDARIZING YOUR TASK LIST

This is called "calendarizing" your task list, and it's the last (and most crucial) step of The Winning The Week Method. Calendarizing is when you take something from your to-do list and block out dedicated time on your calendar to get it done. When you've filled up all the time slots on your calendar, you officially have a plan. Like Pinocchio becoming a real boy, all your work to this point comes together to become a real plan.

Don't be fooled by how simple this sounds. This step is straightforward to understand but, at the same time, frustratingly challenging to do! It's straightforward, because all you have to do is take a task and mark off time on your calendar to do that task. But it's also tricky because in practice it's a heart-wrenching emotional negotiation. It's easy for me to say, "Okay, now choose what will happen this week and what won't happen." But you and I both know it's not that simple.

This is when the music stops and there aren't enough chairs for everyone. This is the moment your wishful thinking hits the hard wall of reality at full speed. Most people avoid this step because they don't want to feel the full impact of reality on their beautiful plan. But not doing this step means you did an excellent job *preparing* to plan but failed to create an actual plan. I'm just as guilty as anyone. Like most people, I had a huge task list in one hand and an empty calendar in the other, and I hoped that one would match the other by the end of the week. Spoiler alert: they never did. I was always short on time and long on tasks. That's why I was overworked—I was chasing the "long tail" of my tasks into infinity.

Reconciling time demand to the fixed supply of time is where the rubber meets the road. It's where you get traction and forward movement. A Ferrari hovering two inches off the ground can have a lot of horsepower, but it will still be going nowhere, spinning its wheels in mid-air until its tires make contact with the pavement. Only then will it zoom forward. Your to-do list touching your calendar is the moment your dreams and goals see forward movement. Call me a productivity nerd if you want, but it's a beautiful thing.

A simple but profound principle of The Winning The Week Method is that when you say you're going to get something done, you also block out a specific time to do it. If you don't do this, your plan is no plan at all.

The goal in this stage of The Winning The Week Method is to make the real choices so that your time supply and time demand match. Simple, but not easy.

A SIMPLE BUT PROFOUND PRINCIPLE
OF THE WINNING THE WEEK METHOD IS
THAT WHEN YOU SAY YOU'RE GOING TO GET
SOMETHING DONE, YOU ALSO BLOCK OUT
TIME TO DO IT.
IF YOU DON'T DO THIS, YOUR
PLAN IS NO PLAN AT ALL.

@DEMIRANDCAREY

ISN'T CALENDARIZING EXCESSIVE?

I realize that most people think that calendarizing your entire week is excessive. I used to feel the same way, so I understand where that thought comes from. Putting every task on your calendar can seem like going overboard. But now I know it's *barely far enough*, which explains why the average person isn't winning their weeks. Even clients who are open to this idea are afraid that this way of operating would just be too rigid for their unpredictable life. I'm going to show you that it's faster and more flexible than you could imagine. It's simply the best way to get it all done and move your agenda forward.

In his book *Indistractable*, productivity expert Nir Eyal puts it this way: "I know many of us bristle at the idea of keeping a schedule because we don't want to be hampered, but oddly enough, we actually perform better under constraints." The way he sees it, eliminating all the white space in your calendar creates a successful model of your week in which you've masterfully met all your responsibilities.

So I'm asking you to hold off judgment until you try it. Rather than making you feel boxed in, you'll find it gives you freedom like you've never felt before. When you calendarize your tasks, you'll know what you need to do by when. That means you'll be more likely to stay on plan and get more done.

Having worked with this technique for over a decade, allow me to point out some reasons it works so well.

Reason #1: You Eliminate Wishful Thinking

Wishful thinking is the scourge of planning. At its essence, wishful thinking is an umbrella term for all the ways we refuse to face the sacrifices that must be made to get things done.

In practice, wishful thinking happens in that moment when we pretend that we can get more done than we actually can. We tell ourselves everything's going to be okay if we "just keep working." But in the long run we can't deny reality: we're not getting the critical things done, and our task list keeps growing. As good as it feels in the moment, it creates a gap between reality and our expectations that grows dangerously large.

Wishful thoughts breed like moths in your pantry. If you see one, I guarantee it's not long before you have an infestation. Wishful thinking tells you, "Don't worry! You'll get to the important project later. Once you're in a better mindset. Or you're in a more focused place. Or you finish some warm-up tasks." But suddenly it's Friday and you ran out of time to get to the important stuff. Cue palm slapping face.

Calendarizing your tasks eliminates the space for wishful thinking. That's why it's such a crucial step and a powerful tool. That's also why we resist it when we don't want to face those sacrifices inherent to modern life.

Reason #2: It Helps Put Your Actions on Autopilot

When it's a dreary Monday morning and your head is still foggy from the weekend, just getting started can be so hard—especially on the big scary tasks that you're feeling avoidance around!

But calendarizing your to-do list helps with this, effectively putting you on autopilot, following the path you've already laid out for yourself. I call this "calendar accountability." I know that sounds strange—how can a calendar hold you accountable? But when you see that today is the only day in the next week when you can get four hours to work on that big project, it puts positive pressure on you to stop delaying and just do it. At that moment, you know that this is the time you've set aside to do that work, and if you slip on it, the task probably won't get done at all that week. It's a powerful nudge (delivered right when you need it the most) to do things when you've scheduled time to do them.

Reason #3: You Always Know What You Should Do Next

Being a knowledge worker is incredibly mentally straining because you have to juggle dozens of tasks and manage new information streams. We make it worse by not having efficient ways to manage all of that. But we make it *unbearable* by second-guessing ourselves! You've probably experienced a week when you had a plan, but you second-guessed the plan. In the end you realized that you would have been better off just following the original plan! The self-sabotage is infuriating, and the loss of energy is exhausting.

But the person who calendarized their task list is never in doubt about what comes next. A quick glance at their calendar always reveals the next right action. That reduces their opportunity for self-sabotage and spares them the mental strain of constantly having to think about what they should do next. Over time, it allows their limbic system to chill out and start trusting the plan, relieving them of that constant panicky feeling.

Reason #4: It Makes Time for Fun Things

Calendarizing your to-do list isn't just about the tasks you'd rather avoid. It's also about making sure there's time for *fun* in your week! Like dinner dates, concerts, and outdoor adventures with the family—whatever you find enjoyable and relaxing. The best things in life don't happen by chance. The more fun you plan into your life, the more fun your life will be.

Calendarizing fun into your life guarantees that you have great things planned for your week, no matter how busy your week is. That ultimately makes your success more sustainable because you have a better balance between work and life. It keeps you loving your life even when things at work are tough. Planning for fun is such an important (but overlooked) element of success that I made it the first step in my five-step calendarizing process.

The Winning The Week Method

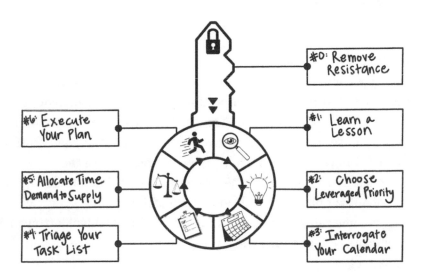

#0: Remove Resistance

#1: Learn a Lesson

#2: Choose Leveraged Priority

#3: Interrogate Your Calendar

#4: Triage Your Task List

#5: Allocate Time Demand to Supply

#6: Execute Your Plan

STEP 5: ALLOCATE TIME DEMAND TO SUPPLY

In this step of The Winning The Week Method, you'll take a few minutes to match demand to supply. Ideally, you should account for all 168 hours of your week in this step. Yes, I said it. That includes the time you spend sleeping, eating, showering, and commuting too! Experts say we should tell our money exactly where we want it to go—why would our time be any different? This is what it means to have extreme ownership over your time.

If you can embrace it, you'll see yourself jump to the next level immediately. But if that idea stresses you out, then dial it back a little. Any calendarizing you do is better than doing nothing at all. So do as much as you're willing to because every little bit helps!

THE LIFEHACK CALENDARIZING PROCESS

Now let's get into how to match your supply to demand so you can finish your plan for the week. Open your calendar of choice and your to-do list, and let's get started.

1. Put in the Good Stuff First

I know your mind wants to go straight to the scariest work projects on your list, but try to resist the temptation to start there. Instead, start by scheduling in the "good stuff": the things that make life enjoyable. This is necessary because in our workaholic society, we push the good stuff off to the end, and it never happens. That's how we end up with "all work and no play" lifestyles. The Winning The Week Method is not just about winning at work—it's about winning the whole enchilada of life.

Here are some categories of activities you might consider slotting in first:
- Self-care: Going to the gym, jogging, getting a massage, or getting a haircut
- Playtime: Hobbies, gaming, going to a movie, or dance lessons
- Social time: Hanging out with the people who matter to you, like friends, family, or work colleagues
- Quiet time: Time to take a walk through nature or sit on the couch and listen to an entire album (one of my personal favorites)
- Creative time: Time to write, paint, draw, or otherwise exercise your creativity
- Significant other time: Especially when you have kids, quality time with a partner seems to evaporate—unless it's in the calendar

If this is a new concept to you, there might be a lot of resistance, so start small. But don't skip this, or I guarantee that (even if you get a lot done) you won't feel like you're winning your weeks.

THE WINNING THE WEEK METHOD IS NOT JUST ABOUT WINNING AT WORK—IT'S ABOUT WINNING THE WHOLE ENCHILADA OF LIFE.

@DEMIRANDCAREY

2. Stack in the Deep Work (Early in the Week)

Next, schedule your Deep Work. Deep Work is any work related to your number one leveraged priority that you set earlier in your planning session. Once you've estimated how much time you think your Deep Work will take, add at least a 30 percent buffer.

If you find that you can't complete your priority in the time you have, take a step back and look at the priority again. You may need to break it down into smaller milestones or reconsider it altogether. This process of briefly revisiting steps you've already covered is what I call "balancing the scales." The goal is to achieve the ideal balance of priority, time supply, and time demand within the limitations of your life. Often this is a recursive process, not a linear one. So don't get upset if you have to double back to some previous steps and re-run them at lightning speed. Personally, I find that thinking about this as a puzzle to be solved makes it fun and engaging.

AVOID THIS ROOKIE MISTAKE

A common rookie error is planning your Deep Work blocks too late in the week. Remember that energy depletes from morning to evening, and from Monday to Friday. This means that, generally speaking, your best energy will be in the mornings early in the week (like Monday and Tuesday). Your worst energy and focus will tend to concentrate at the end of each day and the final days of the week. Knowing that, try to reserve your Mondays and Tuesdays for your priority tasks to ensure that you're matching your best energy to your most important tasks.

That's also why I recommend planning your week and having team meetings on Fridays. That one choice has two significant impacts. First, you'll rest easier on the weekend, knowing that you touched base with your team and there's a plan in place for the coming week. Second, it opens up that critical high-energy time on Monday and Tuesday for your Deep Work.

3. Put in Your UUW Time (No Exceptions!)

If you remember from Chapter 6, UUW stands for Unplanned, Unwanted Work. It's work that will hit your plate, but you don't yet know what it is. UUW time is a placeholder that you put into your calendar to deal with these issues as they come up. Put more simply, it's flex time you know you'll need, but you don't yet know precisely what you'll need it for (yet).

If you have no idea how much time to budget for UUW, start by putting in one hour a day, sometime after 2:00 p.m. The later you schedule this in your day, the better, since you can always pull it forward, but you can't reclaim it when it has passed. It's also wise to schedule your UUW toward the end of the week. Some of my clients reserve all day Friday for UUW that builds up throughout the week.

4. Stuff Shallow Work into the Cracks

So far you've put the good stuff in first, made time for Deep Work, and allocated time for UUW. Now, schedule your Shallow Work tasks (basically, anything that isn't your Deep Work) in the gaps in your schedule. For example, a thirty-minute block of time between two meetings is perfect for Shallow Work. I call this an "orphan time block" because it's been cut off from other blocks of time and rendered unusable for getting Deep Work done. But it's a great time to check your email.

Since you've scheduled your important work early in the week and early in the day, your Shallow Work will tend to fall later in the day or later in the week, when your energy is lower. That's perfect since these tasks don't require your best energy to accomplish. Meetings are nearly always Shallow Work, so schedule them as such: later in the day and later in the week. If you can reschedule any meetings to open up time for Deep Work, do that now. And whenever you schedule new meetings, take first-mover advantage and suggest a time later in the week or later in the day.

5. Keep Going until All of Your Time Supply Has Been Allocated

This last part is where you step back and evaluate the plan. You may decide that the first draft didn't quite succeed. If you don't like what you see, feel free to start over and keep "balancing the scales" until you've got a winning plan.

Go back to the start of the process and (rapidly) rerun The Winning The Week Method. Negotiate with yourself and decide what gets to stay in the plan and what needs to go. This process is akin to a music studio engineer adjusting the sliders until they have the perfect mix.

Calendarizing isn't a clean, linear process. It's recursive, and it can get muddy. Like politics, you will have to make painful concessions and tradeoffs. But just as politics is the "art of what's possible and attainable," you too must let go of your ideal and compromise to achieve the greatest good.

This means you have to:

- Get creative: Are there ways you can think outside of the box to meet your needs and those of the people around you?
- Negotiate powerfully: Are there deadlines you can renegotiate on Shallow Work tasks, or appointments that can get rescheduled?
- Accept reality: Look at your life with zero wishful thinking. Be able to see when a timeline isn't realistic and accept that reality without getting emotional. Accepting life on life's terms is a rare (but valuable) skill.
- Push tasks into next week and even next month: If a task didn't make the cut in this week's calendar, reschedule it for a later date without anguish.
- Communicate this newfound reality to others: If you've made changes that impact your coworkers, family, or clients, now is the time to inform them (especially if the changes are inconvenient or involve bad news). It's hard to disappoint people and have hard conversations, but it's much better to do it in advance than at the last minute.
- Check your perfectionism: Ask yourself what "good enough" looks like and where you can accept a lower level of quality to serve the greater good.

This all takes practice to master but works powerfully, even for first-timers. You'll quickly find that you develop a feel for how to calendarize a week that works for you.

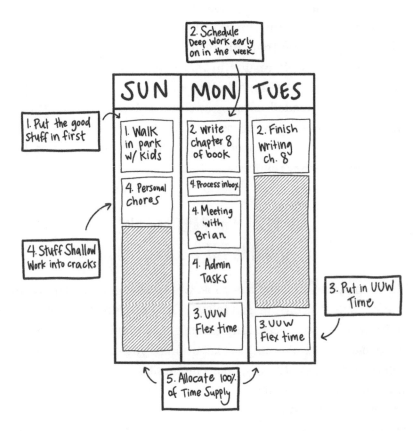

Don't worry if it doesn't work perfectly in the beginning. Often you'll be digging yourself out of a hole and clearing out backlogged tasks that have piled up. That means you might be working mainly on "have to-dos" rather than "want to-dos." Give yourself a grace period of four weeks to clear out backlog, and then I promise you will start finding time for want to-dos rather than only have to-dos.

CHAPTER RECAP

In this chapter, I introduced you to the critical concept of calendarizing your week. Calendarizing is the most crucial step in your planning because it's where your plan actually becomes a plan. It's where you face reality head-on and banish wishful thinking. It's also the one step everyone skips.

While many assume that this technique is overkill and overly restrictive, it's the opposite. It results in more freedom of movement, not less. Calendarizing also solves the "what should I be doing right now?" problem and creates much-needed urgency and motivation. To make this painless, I showed you my five-step process for calendarizing your plan for the week. You can download a cheat sheet for the Lifehack Calendarizing Process at **winningtheweek.com/resources**.

REVIEW OF PART 1 OF THE WINNING THE WEEK METHOD

That completes Part 1 of the book, where I taught you The Winning The Week Method. But as anyone can tell you, it's one thing to create a good plan and quite another to successfully execute that plan. In Part 2, we will focus on how to move from planning to execution so you can bring home the win.

Before we move on, though, take a moment to triumph in a well-designed week. You probably had to make some tough decisions to get this far. And you had to face intense resistance and even fear. But if you've implemented this advice, you also know there's a big payoff! The tension of desperately needing a plan—and living on permanent defense—builds intense pressure. Once that pressure is released, you get flooded with a tremendous sense of relief and joy. That feeling is indescribable! The more you focus on that feeling, the more you start to crave it.

Looking at your beautiful and *totally doable* plan for the week, you'll feel a sense of confidence instead of futility or dread. If you keep this up, you'll set yourself up to hit the ball out of the park every week instead of saying, "Next week is the week."

Will it be perfect? No. In sports, there's always some element of chance that players work hard to mitigate. It's the same with your work. There's always an element of chaos and unpredictability. But when you plan correctly, you'll consistently tip the scales in your favor.

PART 2

EXECUTE
YOUR PLAN

9

STICK TO YOUR PLAN

"The pessimist complains about the wind; the optimist expects it to change; the realist adjusts the sails."

—WILLIAM ARTHUR WARD

ONCE MONDAY MORNING COMES AROUND, THE STARTING BELL OF your weekly game dings, and you're plunged into the chaos of your week. Anything could happen from this point! The only guarantee is that nothing will unfold precisely as you predicted in your plan. This concept is impossibly hard for many to accept, which makes sense because there's a duality built into executing a good plan. On the one hand, a good plan demands specificity—that you wargame your week down to a detailed level. On the other hand, you have to expect that it won't happen that way at all! How can those two contradictions live together in your mind without driving you insane?

While I love the sports and war analogies I've employed so far, allow me to use a different metaphor for this chapter: executing your plan is like navigating the seas. I love that verb—to navigate—because navigating encompasses the act of setting the original course, but also includes all of the minor changes needed to fulfill the original plan and still arrive at the destination.

The sailor starts with a destination and a detailed plan for getting there. But when she sets sail, she is pushed off course in countless ways, big and small, each day. Sometimes it could be her fault for not operating the boat capably. But more likely, these obstacles come from forces she can't hope to control: weather, debris striking the boat, lightning, equipment failure, and pirates (yes, there are still pirates out there). In the face of these setbacks, sailors are constantly making micro-adjustments to their original plan— not to subvert their plan, but to fulfill it.

Sailors understand the crucial value of planning. Talk to any seasoned sailor, and they'll tell you horror stories resulting from a failure to plan: having equipment break and being without spare parts, running into avoidable dangerous weather, or not packing enough critical supplies, among many other scenarios. They also know that no plan can predict what's going to happen at sea. Sailors embrace the contradictions built into excellent planning. They are obsessed with creating detailed plans, *and* they expect the plan to change at any moment. Even when sailing a familiar route, sailors expect every voyage to be remarkably different.

As we move into the specifics of sticking to your plan, I encourage you to adopt the mindset of a sailor. You'll see that all of the tactics I teach you will work better with that approach held firmly in mind. Otherwise, you will struggle needlessly and waste precious energy. Like most tactics in this book, this is easy to say and hard to do. It's natural to feel upset and even angry when things don't go "according to plan." But instead of resisting the unpredictable nature of your reality, I suggest you embrace it with the exhilaration of a sailor. Besides, if plans always worked, then success would be easy—and where's the fun in that? We value our accomplishments precisely because we know how hard they were to achieve. That's the nature of this game you're playing!

"We cannot direct the wind, but we can adjust the sails."
—unknown

Now that you've made a solid plan, it's time to adopt a sailor's mindset and release any expectation that it's going to happen the way you thought it would. Don't think of yourself as "following the plan" but rather as navigating to your final destination using the plan as a guide. Let me share two practices to help you navigate your week. The first is called replanning.

STRATEGY: REPLANNING

In 2020, sailors Riley Whitelum and Elayna Carausu were in a pickle. They were on a voyage across the Atlantic to deliver activist Greta Thunberg to the COP25 conference in Madrid, Spain. Despite intense preparations and a careful study of historical weather patterns, they faced a dangerous weather front forming ahead of them. Whitelum commented:

> We weren't going fast enough. The conditions we were experiencing were slightly different from the forecast. There was wind against the

Gulf Stream, creating bigger, choppier waves than we had anticipated. [My co-captain] and I were working really well together, but we weren't quite getting far enough along our course. At a certain point, the weather people we were talking to said, "There is some serious s**t heading your way. You need to get the hell out of where you are." That meant we needed to change course and head further south. It was pretty dicey for a while, but we managed to get south and get around that crazy storm.

Their triumphant voyage was feted by the global media and was a victory for Thunberg and her cause. "It's the hardest thing I've ever done, but also the thing I'm most proud of," said Whitelum.

This story is an example of planning and replanning done brilliantly. I tell my clients that replanning isn't abandoning the old plan. It's fulfilling it in the face of changing circumstances.

REPLANNING ISN'T ABANDONING THE OLD PLAN. IT'S FULFILLING IT IN THE FACE OF CHANGING CIRCUMSTANCES.

@DEMIRANDCAREY

Take fifteen minutes at the start of each day (or at the end of the day if you prefer) to do a review of how reality has shifted since you set course.

- Evaluate your progress toward your number one priority. Are you on pace to finish that priority by the end of the week? If not, what needs to happen to get you back on track?
- If you got blown off course in a significant way, what has to be sacrificed, traded, or adjusted to get back on course?

Take swift action to shift around work blocks, reprioritize, and push some tasks into the following week. Feel free to cancel or reschedule appointments in light of these changing circumstances, and defer Shallow Work to preserve your deep work time. Remember, this is why you scheduled UUW time into your week—so use it! This gives you essential flexibility when the unexpected happens.

DON'T USE YOUR FREE TIME AS SPILLOVER TIME

I know it's tempting to let work spill into your personal time when you see that you're falling short of your goal. But this puts you on the wrong side of Parkinson's law. Working an extra ten hours in your week won't get you to the end of your task list. Worse, by removing that constraint, you're inviting work to colonize your personal life not just this week, but every week! Like welcoming a vampire into your house, this is a huge mistake. I strongly urge you to remove this option altogether and make it nonnegotiable.

Why? First of all, it's anti-productive. Despite feeling more productive in the short term, as studies have shown, you will slow down to produce less, not more, when you work too much over long periods. Intuitively, this makes sense because, even though you can cover a lot of ground sprinting, in the long run you cover more distance by setting a sustainable pace.

Also, working long hours makes life miserable and does psychological and physical damage that is hard to heal. Take it from me: burnout can do damage that you have to live with for the rest of your life.

But remember that Parkinson's law works in your favor too! When you put limits on your working hours, you will find a way to complete the genuinely vital work in that time frame—and, in the process, set yourself up to lead a sustainable lifestyle.

STRATEGY: PUSHING BACK AGAINST THE CHAOS

In addition to replanning daily, you can take actions throughout the day to combat the effects of UUW. When you get blown off course, here's what to do to mitigate the harm it might do to your plan.

1. Does the UUW Have to Do with Your Top Priority?

If so, welcome the opportunity to move that priority forward! Even if it adds time and work to your plate, it's still getting you closer to your big goal. So lean into it!

2. Is There a Negative Consequence If You Don't Get It Done Right Away?

The consequence of someone being disappointed doesn't cut it. I'm talking about *real* consequences, like losing a client or missing a huge opportunity, not social consequences, like "He'll be disappointed in me." If there's no real consequence, then delay as long as possible.

If there is an unacceptable consequence (like a client threatening to leave), remember to use your UUW time to tackle this. And be sure you're not using "first-tier energy" to tackle it. First-tier energy means those precious hours when you can do your best work. If it's Shallow Work, push it to the end of the day and use "second-tier energy" to deal with it.

3. Negotiate to Push the Deadline Out as Far as Possible

Push hard! Bring the other party's awareness to the fact that their last-minute request is hurting your plans. That will train them to pause and think from your perspective the next time they have this kind of request. Otherwise, you're training them to drop grenades in your lap! This is an opportunity to change the incentives of the people around you.

4. Force Yourself to Use All the Time You're Given

Do not complete tasks earlier than expected. It's easy to think to yourself, *This feels so important, and people are breathing down my neck; I might as well get it done now.* But the opposite is true! If you answer emails right away, you're training people to expect an instant response every time. When you complete tasks days ahead of schedule, you're creating a new baseline that becomes an expectation.

Besides, when people realize they can't get their way instantly, they tend to help themselves more. Napoleon Bonaparte notoriously instructed his secretary not to open letters for three weeks. He then noted with great satisfaction that most issues had been resolved by the time he opened them, saving him the time and energy of sending a response. In the process, he trained the people around him to become less dependent and more resourceful.

The point of these strategies is to never miss an opportunity to give yourself as much space to operate as possible! Whenever and wherever you can, create a buffer zone between yourself and the outside world. When you don't have that buffer zone, you drastically limit your ability to navigate out of dangerous water.

NEVER MISS AN OPPORTUNITY TO GIVE YOURSELF AS MUCH SPACE TO OPERATE AS POSSIBLE.

@DEMIRANDCAREY

My client Rachelle had a boss who liked to send her on "fire drills"—last-minute requests for reports, presentations, and the like. Whenever this happened, she would delay work on it for as long as possible. About 30 percent of the time, her boss would change his mind and either decide he didn't need that report after all or completely change the specifications. This is a great lesson for us all: the same people who are sending UUW your way will often change their minds quickly or find a way to solve the problem themselves. If you get the task done too fast, you risk working on something that isn't useful. By delaying, Rachelle saved herself a tremendous amount of work and frustration. In the process, she subtly retrained her boss not to expect her to jump at a moment's notice.

CHAPTER RECAP

When you plan out your week, you're not *deciding* how the week will happen. You're setting a strong and well-designed *intention*. The difference may be subtle but can completely change your experience of the week. If you feel like you've decided how the week will go, you'll be plagued with frustration and defeatism when reality changes course on you. But when you see your original plan as simply a "first draft" of reality that you aspire to, you'll be expecting the chaos that meets you on Monday morning. In response, you'll be able to make adjustments to change course and still make it to your final destination. Many of my clients describe this slight shift in perspective as game-changing. The amount of energy (and peace of mind) you'll reclaim by not taking that rigid approach is hard to overstate.

Hopefully, you can see that replanning is crucial to winning your week. I've given you some tactics in this chapter to help you replan better and meet those interruptions with confidence. You can download a cheat sheet for replanning and wargaming at **winningtheweek.com/resources**.

But there's much more you can do to execute your plan well. Next, I'll show you the best ways to engineer an environment of focus and block distractions so you can get work done.

10

STOP DISTRACTING YOURSELF

LANA RESTED HER HEAD ON AN EMPTY HOTEL DESK, HER COMPUTER screen blinking back at her.

She was under a deadline to finish a creative brief for a new prospect, but this was more than just another proposal. It was a rare opportunity to take her small business to the next level. If she could land this client, it would mean a *lot* more money and, more importantly, the respect she had been craving since she struck out on her own. This was her "do or die" moment.

So why wasn't she able to focus?

Lana knew how important this was, so she had gotten a hotel room in order to be completely alone, with nothing pulling at her focus. She had created an environment utterly devoid of interruptions: no coworkers, no kids, and no dogs to interrupt her. But it wasn't working.

She reflexively grabbed her phone to check it and then slammed it down. She got up to look at the minibar. She made herself another cup of coffee. But every time she sat down, she found her mind wandering to another distraction:

I wonder what my husband is feeding the kids?

Are there any crucial emails in my inbox?

Maybe I should do more internet research to inspire myself.

We often talk about interruptions as something external. Something that *someone else* is doing to *us*. What might surprise you is that we interrupt ourselves just as much as we are interrupted by others. That means that finding a "flow state" is tricky business, even when a lot is on the line. As Lana found out, not being able to focus can be frustrating to the point of tears. We like to tell ourselves that the fault lies with external distractions, but Lana discovered the hard truth: even when all those distractions are taken away, we still have trouble focusing our minds on the task at hand.

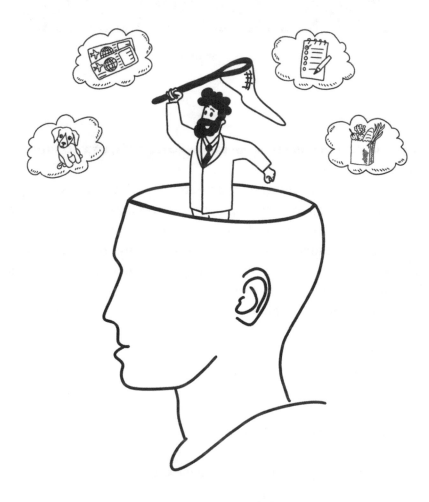

Our ability to simply sit down and focus for long periods has been danger-ously degraded by today's "distraction culture." The past twenty years have been a fertile time for researchers like Dr. Gloria Mark and others studying workplace distraction. Their work has shown beyond any reasonable doubt that distractions kill our productivity, are bad for our mental health, and degrade our ability to focus.

Being able to maintain your focus is absolutely essential to executing the plan that you've laid out. Plus, it gives you an edge over everyone else who is still suffering under the weight of self-inflicted distractions. This chapter will show you a tactic to maintain a focused state where you can really get work done.

This is highly leveraged because if you can hone your focus, you'll find that the sky's the limit in terms of your success. I'm not talking about being able to send hundreds more emails. I'm talking about doing big things—like writing books, building businesses, or getting a PhD. As your ability to focus increases, you'll feel more confident taking on bigger and bigger challenges.

Take the example of one of the most productive people I have ever met: Cal Newport. When I interviewed Newport, he came across as an unassuming computer science professor, but in this case, looks are deceiving. He became the youngest tenured computer science professor at Georgetown University by age thirty-three, which is an impressive feat by itself. But the rest of his résumé is enough to awe anyone. He's published not one, not two, but seven books—all before the age of thirty-nine—many of them *New York Times* best-sellers. In fact, he sold his first book to Random House when he was still an undergraduate in college. Through it all, he has written several blogs with millions of readers and produced a podcast with millions of downloads. One might assume that his work is his whole life, but he has a family with three kids and doesn't work past 5:00 p.m.

Obviously, we're talking about a brilliant individual here—possibly one who has benefited from privileges that aren't afforded to others (I'll include myself in that privileged category). But it's also evident that even if you control for those factors, Newport is an abnormally focused individual. In fact, he wrote an entire book, called *Deep Work*, about how to focus on completing the tasks that create real value in order to succeed in today's economy. So you better believe that when Newport sits down to write a lecture, a chapter of a book, or a blog, he's 100 percent focused on that task for hours at a time.

These kinds of results can seem impossible for the average person who's still getting distracted every three minutes. But the good news is that you can repair your focus rapidly, without any fancy tools or apps. Take my client Richard as inspiration for just how quickly you can restore your ability to focus. He sent me this message after using—for just twenty-four hours—the very same tactic that I'm about to teach you:

> It's 11:40 a.m., and I'm so pumped about all the stuff I've gotten done this morning and yesterday afternoon! I'm totally energized, and I've already logged more than two hours of deep work this morning. Even a week ago, I'd be happy if I logged an hour of deep work in a whole day! Super excited about this progress!

What I love the most about the trick that I'm about to reveal is that it makes focusing feel effortless and even fun!—which means instead of work being a chore that you dread doing, it's actually something you'll lean into. And that's because it leverages our brain's completely natural and wildly effective built-in focus mechanism: our love of playing games.

GAMIFYING YOUR WORK BLOCKS

Almost all mammals learn and develop by playing games. It's the way each of us learned as a child. When a child is playing a game, they are preternaturally focused and engaged—but they're also delighted—sometimes to the point where they're giggling with glee. Evolution gave us a powerful positive feedback loop for developing ourselves by doing challenging things. Check this against your own experience. Can you remember what it feels like to be totally engrossed in a game? Have you ever gotten so lost in a game that you lost track of time or shouted out with glee? This is the power that games have over us.

But as we get older, we play games less and less until all traces of fun have been completely stripped from our life. We have a solemn cultural attitude toward work, and games don't fit into that mold. Games for adults are considered childish at worst and reserved for downtime at best. If anyone at work seems to be having too much fun, people will naturally assume "they're not taking it seriously"—or maybe they aren't working hard enough.

We're paying the price for this solemn attitude in degraded performance. Biologically, we're still hunter-gatherers who work and learn through play, but we're trying to force ourselves to execute our work like robots. It feels hard because we're working against our biology, not with it. But what would happen if we started playing at work? What if, instead of dreading work, we looked forward to work? What if we got so engrossed in our work that time got away from us or we occasionally shouted out with glee?

This is called gamification, where we bring the mechanics of play into our work. I'm going to show you a short game that I created that kills six birds with one stone:

- It helps you get highly focused.
- It enables you to work much faster.
- It shows you how to reclaim those orphan time blocks.
- You make fewer mistakes.
- Deep Work feels almost effortless.
- You start enjoying work a whole heck of a lot more!

I call it the Sticky Focus Game. Put your phone away because all you'll need is a pack of sticky notes (like Post-it notes) and a pen.

Here's how to play:

1: Open Your Calendar and Look at Your Schedule

Add up all of your open blocks of time for today. That means everything that isn't already claimed by a meeting or commitment. Thirty minutes here, an hour there. You might see an orphan time block in between meetings— count those too. This total represents the time in your day where you can work on something without distraction. Add it all up to see how much time you have to move the ball forward today.

2: Lay Out One Sticky Note per Hour of Availability

Let's say you have three hours of available time today (the rest is committed to other things). You'll take three sticky notes and slap them down in front of yourself. Each of these sticky notes represents an hour-long work block where you can get focused work done. If you have a thirty-minute open block instead of a full hour, you can rip a sticky note in half to represent that smaller time block.

What you've done here is created a *time currency*. Just like a dollar bill represents one unit of money, each of these sticky notes is now a physical representation of a discretionary block of your time. It's easier to manage your time this way because now you can see it, touch it, and manipulate it in physical space.

3: Write Your Most Essential Tasks on These Sticky Notes

Now look at your task list and identify the big things that absolutely have to get done with these three focused hours. Ideally, they will be tasks that get you to your number one goal for the week, but you can use your judgment. Go ahead and write those tasks down on the sticky notes. If you have more than three hours' worth of tasks, you can feel free to put more sticky notes out—just know that they probably won't all happen today. They will need to bleed over into sometime later in the week. But it never hurts to have a couple in reserve in case you get stuck on a task or work through a task faster than expected.

4: Order the Sticky Notes from Most Important to Least Important

Next, you're going to rearrange the sticky notes in front of you in the order of their importance. Though they all might seem equally important, some will be more leveraged than others. Go back and review the chapter on setting leveraged priorities if you're having difficulty choosing. Once you have your sticky notes placed in order of importance, move to the next step.

5: Set a Timer for Fifty Minutes

Next, you fire the starting gun, and the game begins! Pull out a kitchen timer and set it to fifty minutes. This is where the gamification really kicks in. The objective of this game is to focus only on this task until the alarm goes off. You're trying to shut out the world and allow your brain to focus only on the task at hand. I joke with my clients that if a war broke out, you wouldn't know until you finished the work block. That's how focused you're trying to be.

Don't worry about whether you'll finish the task in precisely the time allotted—that's beside the point. Just try to put as big a dent in the task as you can for fifty minutes. If you can do that, I promise you'll be happy with the quality and speed of your work regardless of whether you complete it or not. If you're familiar with the concept of "pomodoros," this is similar but with a much heavier emphasis on gamification. You're playing against yourself to see how deeply you can focus for fifty minutes.

6: Turn Off Distractions

To succeed, you'll have to block all distractions and potential interruptions. Set your phone to Do Not Disturb, turn off your email notifications, and close Facebook and TikTok. Consider moving to a quieter room in your house or a deserted conference room at work. Maybe put a sign on your door telling people not to come in for the next fifty minutes. Everything that could be a potential distraction has to get nipped in the bud so you can set yourself up for success.

I'm constantly challenging myself to get each work block done without interruptions from either internal or external sources. I wear big over-the-ear headphones so people aren't as likely to interrupt me. I turn off my WhatsApp, close any browsers that don't relate to my tasks at hand, and put both my computer and phone on Do Not Disturb.

It wouldn't be a game if you couldn't lose, right? Since your goal is to focus without getting distracted in any way, "losing" means allowing yourself to get distracted. If you lose your focus, you lose that sticky session. When you stay focused, you win. Some people go easier on scoring themselves, but I find that keeping the challenge level high really makes it fun and keeps me engaged.

Once the alarm goes off, you're done! If you focused for fifty minutes straight, you will have noticed a massive jump in your productivity. Trust me, the feeling isn't subtle...you'll feel like you've gotten more done in an hour than you usually do in four hours of work. Clients who "lose" this game (meaning they weren't perfectly focused the entire time) often tell me that they're *still* so much more productive compared to when they aren't even trying. So even when you lose, you win!

Although the point is not to finish the task, at some point, you will eventually complete your task during a work block. When you do, crumple the sticky note and put it in a bowl in front of you. That growing pile of crumpled stickies will serve as a physical representation of your output. The problem with knowledge work is that you can't touch it or see it when it's completed, making it hard to feel a sense of accomplishment. Now you'll have a bowl full of these little crumpled-up stickies on your desk to represent the work you did this week.

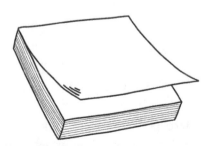

INCOMPLETE

ALL DONE!

7: Give Yourself a Reward

In between the Sticky Focus Game sessions you'll have a ten-minute break. No matter how well (or how poorly) you feel you did, you must take this time to reward yourself. I like to give myself a little guilt-free time to watch a short YouTube video or pop into the kitchen for a snack.

Whatever you do, don't skip the reward because you don't think you deserve it. Rewards aren't about deserving something. They're about creating a positive reinforcement loop. Imagine trying to train a puppy without treats. It's impossible because rewards are the key to reinforcing good behavior. Just like cute little puppies, our brains need rewards to reinforce new behaviors. If your aim is to train yourself to focus intensely, you must reward yourself. Every single time.

Plus, frequently resting your brain is crucial to maximizing the overall amount of work you can do in a day. Just as bodybuilders rest between heavy sets, you should rest your brain between intense work sessions. You'll be surprised how quickly you tire out from mental exhaustion if you work straight through for several hours with no breaks.

SUPERCHARGED STICKIES

If you want to take it to another level, here's a bonus tip for your Sticky Focus Game: supercharge the game by using blue stickies for Shallow Work and pink stickies for Deep Work (or whatever two colors you want). The pink stickies represent the truly meaningful work (your Deep Work). Maybe that's something that you're procrastinating on or that's outside of your comfort zone (which is typically your most leveraged work). Imagine that you completed one thing outside your comfort zone every day. How much faster would you reach your goals? The blue stickies represent your Shallow Work, the regular work that has to be done to maintain the status quo.

LANA REVISITED

Lana sent me an SOS from her hotel room, explaining what was happening. I showed her the Sticky Focus Game and challenged her to a competition: the person who could get the most sessions done before 5:00 p.m. would buy the other one a Starbucks gift card. She accepted my challenge.

I kept getting fun messages from her throughout the day:

> First sticky session complete!
>
> Wow two sessions in two hours.
>
> Third session and I'm HOT right now.
>
> WHO IS THIS PERSON I don't recognize her lol.

By the end of the day, Lana had completed five sticky sessions (and she beat me, by the way). More importantly, she finished off most of the work she originally thought she needed three days to complete.

> Signing off for the day, but seriously THANK YOU. I am flabbergasted. Holy moly that was exactly what I needed today. I think I'm going to cry some tears of joy in the kitchen right now.

CHAPTER RECAP

Planning your week is useless if you can't trust yourself to sit down and execute that plan. The ability to block distractions and focus on one thing at a time for extended periods is a crucial skill for doing this. The problem is not just outside of us. Even if you could manage to clear out all external distractions (which is unlikely), you'll still face the internal distractions that sabotage your focus.

The key is "gamifying" your work. Once you bring gamification to your work, you'll be working with your biology instead of against it. That shift will allow you to work much faster, make fewer mistakes, and enjoy your work a whole heck of a lot more.

For most people, capturing focus is like chasing a butterfly—tricky and elusive. But now you have a tool for consistently accessing a state of deep focus: the Sticky Focus Game. You can download the cheat sheet for playing the Sticky Focus Game at **winningtheweek.com/resources**. It summarizes the steps for easy reference when you sit down to play.

11

BLOCK EXTERNAL DISTRACTIONS

DID YOU KNOW THAT THE AVERAGE PROFESSIONAL WORKS IN A focused state for just *three minutes and five seconds* before getting interrupted? Needless to say, three minutes is an insanely short amount of time to concentrate on anything, much less the critical work we need to do each day. It's no wonder we find it so hard to get things done!

This observation comes from Dr. Gloria Mark, a professor at UC Irvine and an expert on the workplace. Mark has done groundbreaking research revealing the shocking number of interruptions we face during the workday. Disturbingly, Mark's research shows it takes twenty-three minutes to get back to the level of focus we had before we were interrupted. That "distraction hangover" happens when we have to reorient ourselves to the task we were pulled away from ("What was I doing again?"). Like an old computer rebooting, we need time to warm back up to an intensely focused state.

These two observations are terrifying when taken together. If it takes twenty-three minutes to get focused, and we're interrupted every three minutes, that means we're never fully concentrating on anything.

As covered in the last chapter, a big part of the solution is to stop distracting yourself. But equally important is preventing outside distractions from reaching you. I call this "re-engineering your environment": redesigning your environment to remove distractions coming from external sources. As you can imagine, this is hyper-leveraged because it only has to be done once, and then it prevents those distractions from ever occurring in the future.

Even better, you don't have to learn a complicated technology, buy a new app, or take a costly supplement. You're not adding anything; you're subtracting. You're looking to simplify your environment, not complexify.

BLOCKING EXTERNAL DISTRACTIONS

The majority of my clients' external distractions come from three main sources:

- Messages
- Notifications
- People coming into their space to interrupt them

I define messages broadly. Since every application seems to have its own messaging feature these days, instant messages could come from dozens of places, like email, WhatsApp, Slack, Facebook Messenger, and the list goes on. Similarly, I define notifications broadly, because they come from all sources too. While they usually appear on your phone, tablet, or desktop, these days they can appear via smartwatch or home speakers. Finally, when I talk about people coming into your space, I invite you to think about that broadly as well. In addition to walking into your room, people can project themselves digitally via a call or video conference request.

While you could try to tackle these distractions one by one, this is like playing Whac-A-Mole—when you knock one down, two others pop up. It's far better to reimagine your environment in the ideal state: what would a "win-win" situation look like, where everyone was better off? This would mean you would get more time to focus, and at the same time everyone else could get more of what they need from you. I call this a "win-win" work environment.

The primary tool, by far, for achieving this is a thoughtful communication policy. It's a clear policy for how others can communicate with you to create a win-win for all parties. You win by not getting distracted and reclaiming your time and focus. They win because they know when they'll get access to you (instead of having to drop by your office ten times a day trying to find you).

Making a communication policy can seem daunting, but I assure you it's easier than trying to hang on to the status quo. Current office communications are a complete disaster. Think of a massive interstate highway system without rules, signs, or lane lines. Imagine how many accidents would occur if we didn't have basic rules of the road when driving. Can you picture it? That's what communication is like in today's workplaces. It's a free-for-all! Everyone is emailing, dropping by, and scheduling meetings willy-nilly. There are no rules, and as a result, there are massive pileups and delays everywhere.

The point of a communication policy is to create those rules of the road by teaching people how to reach you and how not to. When done right, everyone can still get what they need from you, and you can keep yourself focused on what matters. I used to be an advocate for company-wide communication policies, but I've realized since that there are problems with a top-down approach:

1. Most companies haven't created one (and won't anytime soon), leaving individuals and teams to fend for themselves.

2. Many top-down policies are poorly enforced, so everyone ignores them, and that degrades institutional trust.
3. Some groups and individuals genuinely need a communication policy customized to their unique situation, like sales or IT.
4. You're more likely to embrace a policy that you had a hand in creating than a policy that was forced upon you.

For these practical reasons, you should take the initiative and establish your own communication policy.

EXPECTATIONS ARE EVERYTHING

A good communication policy strikes a bargain. Even if the counterparty never explicitly agrees to that bargain, they are agreeing *implicitly*. At its core, a communication policy says to the world, "If you do X, you'll get Y." This bargain gives the sender an incentive to cooperate *and* gives them the most important thing they need from you: certainty. Let me make a controversial statement that most people disagree with at first: People don't need an instant response from you. They need absolute certainty about *when* you'll respond.

People disagree with that statement because (in their lived experience) *it sure does seem that people need an instant response*. A major part of this misconception comes from anxiety. People are worried that you haven't seen their email, and experience tells them that if you didn't respond within forty-eight hours, you will probably never respond at all. Sadly, in most cases they're right. That's why people hound you for a timely response, because late usually means never.

It's also why they feel the need to send you endless check-ins and follow-ups. They hate having to do that (I'm sure you do too) because it's incredibly annoying and stressful to have to hound someone to get a response. It creates extra anxiety and shifts responsibility onto them instead of the person who should have it. So almost all of the behaviors that seem to imply that people need an instant response are just the result of people trying to create certainty around *when* they will get a response.

PEOPLE DON'T NEED AN INSTANT RESPONSE FROM YOU. THEY NEED ABSOLUTE CERTAINTY ABOUT *WHEN* YOU WILL RESPOND.

@DEMIRANDCAREY

My personal communication policy proves that it's certainty, not speed, that people are craving. In my policy, I tell people that I will reply to their email within five business days (effectively a week or more). You might think that's quite a long time, but actually people love it because it guarantees my response time. That gives them certainty that it's on my plate, so they can stop worrying about it and relax. And by publicly stating my policy, I'm also holding myself accountable to adhere to that response time. Believe me, the rare times when I have violated it, people have called me on it. So it governs my behavior just as much as it governs theirs.

Let me acknowledge the elephant in the room before we move on. Every industry and role will have different needs and expectations around response times. If you're in sales or customer service, response time is paramount. But even in those industries, my clients have created win-win communication policies that helped them reclaim their focus and execute their plan for the week. So although everyone gets to figure this out for themselves, no one is exempt from taking ownership of their communication policy.

CREATING YOUR COMMUNICATION POLICY

So what is a communication policy exactly? It's a radically simple document that lays out the best way for you to communicate with others and for them to communicate with you in turn. It can be as simple as this:

> To best direct my energy to high-priority projects, I will be checking and responding to emails twice a day, at 10:00 a.m. and 4:00 p.m. If you need something from me urgently outside those times, please call me at [my number]. Please try to avoid using instant messages wherever possible. Email is always the best way to reach me.

This communication policy is barely a paragraph but manages to include all the essential elements:

- It tells you when you'll be batching your communications so you can focus and get real work done.
- It tells everyone else the best times to reach you and when to expect a response from you (approximately 10:00 a.m. and 4:00 p.m.).
- It offers an emergency option as a steam valve. In this case, your phone number. And don't worry—people will use this less than 1 percent of the time. It's mostly there to ease their anxiety.
- It cuts off an entire communication channel (instant messages) and redirects to your preferred channel (email). Of course, you can choose any preferred channel you wish, but I like email because it's widely used and makes organizing a large volume of communications easier.

A person following this simple policy would create significant periods of time during the day to concentrate and get important work done. And they would give their coworkers and stakeholders a high level of certainty around how and when to reach them.

You can add more to your policy, but be careful. Everything you add should respond to specific recurring "collisions" that happen frequently on your communications highway. For example, as project lead, my client Sarah was being cc'd on every single email that her team sent to each other. This made it impossible to know if her input was actually needed or not. The only way to know for sure was to read every email she received, and she got over three hundred emails per day! So she created this communication policy:

Did you know that only 12 percent of the emails I receive include a specific action for me to do? So that I don't miss anything important from you...

- If your email requires me to take a specific action, please put me in the "To" field so I know a specific action is needed.

- Any emails where I am cc'd or bcc'd will only get a cursory review once weekly but will not receive a response.

- If it's urgent, call immediately at [my number]. You can call three times in a row to break through my Do Not Disturb.

Thanks!

—Sarah

This small change allowed her to skip past all the emails she was cc'd on and instead "batch review" those emails once per week, dramatically reducing her time spent on email. It also helped her quickly see which correspondence was time-sensitive or specifically required her attention, saving energy she had previously wasted wading through low-priority emails.

My client Harvey had a different type of recurring communication collision: his stakeholders were inviting him to far too many meetings. He spent 85 percent of his work hours in meetings, which meant that his actual work bled into his personal time. Since his coworkers couldn't see the aggregate impact of their meeting requests, each individual meeting request felt necessary and justified. So he created the following communication policy:

Due to the extraordinarily high volume of meeting requests I receive, please think twice before inviting me to a meeting. Here are some better ways to get what you need from me on a much faster timeline:

- Drop in during my office hours (daily from 12:00 p.m. to 1:00 p.m.) with your question.

- Allow me to send you a screencast status update to answer your questions (in place of attending your meeting).

- Send me the meeting recording, whereupon I commit to review and send my feedback to you within two business days.

If you absolutely must invite me to a meeting:

- Make sure to attach a meeting agenda to your meeting invite (I will automatically decline meeting requests without an agenda).

- Do not schedule meetings during my appointments titled "Work Block" because that time is set aside to work on time-sensitive deliverables.

- Try to avoid scheduling me for meetings on Monday or Tuesday or before noon Eastern Time, as this is my Deep Work time.

Thanks in advance for your understanding! The purpose of this policy is to get you the best work product and the most responsive version of me.

These collisions don't have to be digital. You can help people who share the same physical space understand how to interact with you—even kids and spouses! My client Lizzie is a pastor who was suffering from never-ending interruptions. The prior pastor had set an expectation that anyone could walk into the pastor's office at any time, a habit that continued when Lizzie started her tenure there. It quickly destroyed her productivity and robbed her of the ability to structure her workflow.

So she created this policy and pasted it outside her office door:

!READ BEFORE KNOCKING
OR ENTERING!

I am easily distracted and love conversation, so I have to work hard to focus while in the office. If my door is closed, that's the signal that I'm focusing and getting important work done. But I open my door and take a break for the last ten minutes of every hour. That's the best time to pop in on me. **During those breaks, I promise to give you my full attention.**

Here's what to do if I'm busy:

- Quick question or need to check something? → Email me.

- Something vital needs handling by the end of the day? → Email me with "URGENT" in the subject line.

- A "life or death" emergency that requires me to drop everything? → Knock on the door OR call me if I'm not in the office. Call three times in a row to break through my Do Not Disturb.

    * Exceptions to the rule: the District Superintendent, the Bishop, or my mother.

- Someone called? → Take a message, and tape it to my door.

- Someone dropped something off? → Put it in my box.

- Need to ask me something before taking action? → Wait till I'm on break.

- Someone arrived and wants to talk to me? → Have them wait till I'm on break, or schedule a meeting.

Thank you for helping me serve you better!

—Pastor Lizzie

Notice how she makes it a win-win by taking frequent breaks and promising to give people her full, undivided attention during those breaks. She also gives her stakeholders multiple options to get what they need without bothering her. She tells them how to handle specific scenarios that she has seen them struggle with in the past. And most importantly, she gives them multiple options for self-selecting the urgency of their message. That implies she trusts that they will make the right decision and not abuse that privilege.

Let me show you what this can look like when taken even further. As co-founder and head coach at my company, I receive a large volume of outreach that I can't possibly respond to. Because of this, I have a detailed communication policy embedded in an auto-responder that goes out to everyone who sends me an email. Here's what people receive from me when they email me:

SUBJECT: [Auto-Reply] Thanks for your message! Check out these resources while you wait for a response.

Thanks for writing to me! You deserve a fast response, but I also need time to do Deep Work. To resolve this conflict, I created this communication policy:

- **Current customers:** If you have admin questions about any of our offerings, please email Paul at paul@lifehackmethod.com.

- **Interested in our productivity coaching?** Learn more at https://lifehackmethod.com.

- **Partnerships:** If you're interested in partnering with us, please email Carey at carey@lifehackmethod.com.

When contacting me:

- Please note that my average email response time is five business days.

- If your issue can't wait that long, please put URGENT in the subject line, and I will respond within one to two business days.

- If this is an emergency (e.g., life or death), please put EMERGENCY in the subject line, and I will respond as soon as I see it. Kindly do not abuse these privileges.

- Please don't reach out to me through any other channels (like LinkedIn, Facebook, Voxer, etc.). Even if I have an account on that service, I rarely check it. Email is the best way to reach me.

- Given the large volume of incoming communications, I'm not able to guarantee a response. If I never respond to your email, please don't take offense. If it's vitally urgent, feel free to resend.

To explore our productivity content, check out:

- Our media page: lifehackmethod.com/media/

- Free workshops: lifehackmethod.com

- YouTube: youtube.com/c/lifehackbootcamp

That is the Cadillac of communication policies. It gives the sender options to go around me to get what they need, tailored to the most frequently asked questions I receive via email.

- It tells *me* what I need to do to hold up my end of the bargain (i.e., respond no later than five business days).
- It tells the sender when they can expect a response from me.
- It offers not one but *two* emergency options to get a quicker response.
- It cuts off all channels of communication except for email.

I admit that this is a maximalist approach, which I can do because it's my business. You may not have that same authority. I included my communication policy to inspire you, not scare you. Remember that anything you do is better than nothing when blocking external distractions! Just know that in the six years I've had this policy, I've never *once* had a grumble or complaint. Neither have any of my clients who have implemented nearly identical policies. But I have received hundreds of emails that simply say, "This is genius. I am stealing this communication policy." And in recent years I've started seeing this policy *come back at me* in other people's auto-responders!

THE BIG OBJECTION TO A COMMUNICATION POLICY

"I'm worried about how my stakeholders will respond to my communication policy."

A common objection to creating a communication policy is that people are scared to put it out there. They are afraid (and in some cases, rightly so) that they will be attacked or criticized for daring to implement any rules of the road. There's always a risk associated with doing something no one else is doing in your office—or rather that no one is doing *yet*, because many of my clients' communications policies are quickly adopted by their teams.

I'm happy to tell you that this fear is a mile wide and paper thin. In almost ten years of coaching thousands of clients, I have not had one (not one!) experience of a bad reaction to rolling out a communication policy. However, here are some tips to help smooth the rollout of your communication policy.

Tip #1: Always Explain How This Benefits Them

Many people will naturally assume that a communication policy is a power play: a way to take something away from them so that you win and they lose. To counteract this bias, you'll need to explain how the new policy benefits them. Often that only requires one well-crafted sentence. Here's a quick example:

"I saw an important email of yours got buried under low priority stuff. So I'm implementing this policy to make sure that never happens again!"

This puts the emphasis on them receiving the best-quality service from you. You don't have to tell people how your communication policy benefits you, because they will automatically assume you're taking care of your own interests. So just leave that out.

Tip #2: Include Data That Explains Why You're Making This Change

Data is a powerful way to inform people why you need to change now without appealing to emotions. Here's a bad example of an emotional appeal:

"I'm getting way too many emails that have nothing to do with me, and I'm drowning having to process them all."

Although this is undoubtedly true, it's unprofessional and opens you up to being characterized as weak or a complainer. Here's how Sarah, from our earlier example, framed that argument using data:

"Did you know that only 12 percent of the emails I receive include a specific action for me to do?"

Notice how this data gets the reader interested. *Oh really? Wow, that's interesting!* And it seamlessly transitions to the change Sarah is going to make: *If it's something actionable and important, put me in the "To" field.*

Tip #3: Take It to Your Boss First

Before you roll out a communication policy to everyone in your organization, take it to your boss as a courtesy. Make sure to explain where this is coming from and, most importantly, how they and the rest of the team will benefit in a big way. They may quiz you about it and request specific changes or modifications. Your boss may even ask that you share it discreetly instead of publicly, which leads to my next suggestion.

Tip #4: Think about Sharing One-on-One

It's better in some cases to share your communication policy directly with your team members individually or in small group settings. I suggest adding it as an agenda item at the end of a small meeting or casual encounter. That feels more personal and invites less scrutiny. It also allows you to answer questions and address concerns they may have. After initial misgivings about sharing her communication policy, my client Ananya realized that just four people represented over 70 percent of her communications. So she simply sat those four down and got their buy-in personally.

Tip #5: It's Still Important to Have It, Even If You Can't Share It

My client Martina couldn't muster the courage to share her communication policy. I advised her to write it anyway as an exercise in visualizing the best rules of the road. After a couple weeks, I asked her what she thought of it. She replied:

"I still think it's been so helpful. Even just creating rules of the road for myself has been clarifying. I'm not living out of my inbox all day anymore. I don't know if I'm imagining it, but I feel like people are picking up on it without me saying anything."

So even though it works best when shared with your stakeholders, a communication policy still has tremendous value even if you never share it with anyone.

Again, communication policies are something that people have a lot of fear around but turn out to be a big nothing-burger. I encourage you not to overthink it. Lest you think my clients have easygoing work environments, I purposefully chose client examples from extremely demanding industries for this chapter: international banking, legal compliance, and interpersonal service work.

Sarah works in compliance with an international bank. She puts it best: "No one freaked out, and not one single person has pulled the 'emergency cord' (calling or texting me) since April 2020!" Amazing, right? Sarah had previously been terrified of rolling out her policy, but it's revealing that no one had any objection. Despite inviting coworkers to call her in case of emergency, no one has done it in over a year. But including that option gives them peace of mind, knowing that they can get ahold of her if they need to. And the benefit to Sarah has been enormous. She's gone from processing email for over fifteen hours a week to less than one hour a week!

I'm giving you a template communication policy to use as a jumping-off point. You can access it at **winningtheweek.com/resources**. You'll see three options you can use to start writing your communication policy.

CHAPTER RECAP

Blocking external distractions is vital for reclaiming your focus and executing a winning plan for the week. We've been trained to think that we live in a zero-sum world when it comes to working: that for you to win, someone else has to lose. After years steeped in this thinking, it can be hard to believe anything else. I promise you that it is not true. You can create an environment where everyone is far better off than before.

A communication policy is the most straightforward tool you can use to block distractions and create a win-win work environment. In this chapter, I invited you to observe the communication collisions that pull your focus away from your work, and then create a policy that is simple to understand and has a clear value proposition for everyone involved.

Despite everything we've covered, there's still a problem. No matter how efficiently you operate, you'll face days and weeks where you lose your willpower and determination. Like a sailor hitting the doldrums, it will feel like a slog just to show up to work and do the bare minimum. How can you push through these stagnant weeks when you have no motivation?

Next, let's talk about accountability because that's your secret weapon for getting through the inevitable doldrums.

12

DESIGN POWERFUL
ACCOUNTABILITY

IN 1954 ROGER BANNISTER BECAME THE FIRST MAN TO RUN A MILE in under four minutes, and a popular worldview shattered.

Conventional wisdom had held that it was physically impossible to run a mile in less than four minutes. Elite runners had been looking to break that barrier since 1886, but none had succeeded. So it's easy to see why a belief permeated the running world that the four-minute mark was a barrier that humans couldn't cross. After all, the human speed barrier has to lie somewhere, right?

But Bannister's achievement is not the most fantastic thing about this story. What boggles the mind is that just forty-six days later, Australian John Landy beat the record again. Over the course of that next year, many other runners would repeatedly break the barrier. Somehow, after standing for over fifty years, the record was surpassed by multiple elite runners in less than one year. Clearly Bannister didn't have some talent that no one else possessed. Rather, his victory had removed the false belief that it wasn't possible and, in the process, unleashed the competitive instincts of other elite runners. The moment people discovered that the barrier could be punctured, they shifted their beliefs and blew past the mental blockage. In the end, the biggest barrier to the four-minute mile wasn't physical—it was mental.

SOCIAL PRESSURE IS THE HIDDEN INGREDIENT TO SUCCESS

Although our ego hates to acknowledge it, our social environment has a tremendous influence on our ability to succeed. We desperately want to think of ourselves as the captain of our ship. However, the environment we put ourselves in shapes our beliefs, and our beliefs put a ceiling on what we can accomplish. This phenomenon is classic "social pressure," defined by the American Psychological Association as "the exertion of influence on a person or group by another person or group. Like group pressure, social pressure includes rational argument and persuasion...calls for conformity...and direct forms of influence, such as personal attacks on the one hand and promises of rewards or social approval on the other."

An example of this is the social pressure that influenced me to go to college. As a child, my family constantly talked about me going to college. It was casually understood that I would attend college (even though only one person in my family tree had gone before me). The only question was which one. Contrast that with my close friend Matt's family, who immigrated from rural Vietnam. For them, a college education could be attained only by the rare few. So it's no wonder that Matt didn't attend college, despite being a smart guy and a great student.

Social pressure can create radically different outcomes. It influenced me to go to college to fit in with my family's expectations. But for Matt, social pressure convinced him that college was beyond his reach.

THE LIMITS OF WILLPOWER

Today's culture fixates on the individual's ability to steer their ship. We celebrate discipline and willpower precisely because it reinforces what we want to believe: that we are in control. As such, a lot has recently been made about growing one's willpower. Willpower is likened to a muscle, and people reason that the more we train it, the bigger it becomes.

Sadly, if willpower is a muscle, it's a tiny muscle. I joke with my clients that willpower is like your index finger. You can strengthen it, but it's never going to lift much. Having coached thousands of people, I can say with absolute confidence that willpower isn't enough. Not even close. It's such a scarce resource that it will give out, usually sooner than later. In my coaching, I have seen a consistent trend with high performers. They don't use their limited willpower to fight against the current; they change their environment so that they can swim with the current.

In his book *Willpower Doesn't Work*, Benjamin Hardy makes the case that our environment, not force of will, creates our success. He argues that by placing yourself in the right environment, you're creating positive social pressure to perform. He calls these "enriched environments" and describes them as environments with:

- High difficulty (or challenge level)
- High novelty (or interest level)
- High consequence for poor performance
- High social pressure
- High investment

Hardy asserts that these kinds of environments create "eustress" (literally meaning "good stress"). Eustress is a beneficial type of stress that comes from being pushed outside of our comfort zone, but not too far. The result is a feeling of excitement, accomplishment, and meaning.

In other words, Hardy asserts that people performing at their highest level aren't doing so because of their superior willpower. Instead, they are getting committed to something with real consequences in a big way and placing themselves in challenging (but exciting) environments with other people pursuing that same goal.

When people say they need to "get some accountability" in their life, they generally mean that kind of positive social pressure.

INTRINSIC OR EXTRINSIC MOTIVATION?

The problem is that most accountability environments fail. As market research for my coaching business, I interviewed hundreds of members of various programs that advertise accountability. That investigation revealed a surprising result: the vast majority of their attempts to "get accountability" had failed miserably. Curious, I dove deeper, conducting in-depth interviews exploring the few accountability environments that had worked, and the many that had failed.

The most common type of failed accountability provided negative reinforcement via punishment or a fear-based system. Sadly many people are attracted to this kind of accountability, thinking, *I just need someone to force me to do what I need to do!* That type of reinforcement can work well for a very brief period, because our built-in fear response programming is strong. But it backfires in short order as your lizard brain kicks into overdrive to avoid the source of that pain and fear. (Revisit Chapter 3 for a refresher on how mental resistance builds and ultimately sabotages your progress.)

The only sustainable form of accountability happens when your environment *boosts* your intrinsic motivation. Intrinsic motivation is a desire to take action that feels like it comes from deep within you rather than from an external source. Though this may appear to contradict the concept of positive social pressure (which comes from outside yourself), it does not. The environments that create intrinsic motivation exert such subtle pressure on you that you ultimately believe the change is *coming from inside you.* That's the magic of great accountability: you don't feel forced to do it; *you want to do it.* So yes, you need the external stimulus. But when done correctly, it feels like it comes from within you. This is the duality built into great accountability, and it also explains why it's so hard to create these environments.

When successful, this type of accountability is long-lasting and creates a cycle of achievement that gets more powerful over time. Like a fish in a fast-flowing river, you can think of accountability as the flow of water that carries you along. Although you *feel* like a free agent, in truth the environment exerts a subtle but powerful influence on you. Put another way, when your environment values what you value, you find yourself doing more of those things. And when the current is pulling you along, you find it easier and easier to hit goals that used to be difficult or even impossible.

Wanting to create the magic of intrinsic accountability, I carefully analyzed the accountability structures that effortlessly propelled their participants to their highest level. The result was a simple model that I call the Four Layers of Accountability. It's the secret sauce behind our business success with the Lifehack Method and something that anyone can use to create powerful accountability in their life.

THE FOUR LAYERS OF ACCOUNTABILITY

My most exciting finding was that high-functioning accountability environments didn't rely on just one mode of accountability. They engaged in multiple modes at the same time. Participants are swaddled in multiple layers of accountability so they are tightly wrapped.

Why would that be beneficial? Because we try to wiggle out of accountability in our weaker moments! Let's get real—as much as we like to talk about wanting accountability, there's moments when we try to escape. For example, in a coaching relationship (with just one layer of accountability), wiggling out is as easy as ignoring your coach's calls and emails. But the folks we interviewed described four-layered accountability as "impossible to escape" and "all-encompassing." They also spoke in amazement about how these environments made them feel like they had more willpower, motivation, and belief in themselves.

Let's break down each layer. As you read the rest of this chapter, I want you to think about a past accomplishment that blew you away and ask yourself: Which of these layers of accountability were present to reinforce your discipline and determination to get that amazing result?

THE BAR RAISER

The first layer of accountability is what I call a Bar Raiser. This is a person who sets the bar high for you—much higher than you would set it yourself. Together with you, they create a space of elevated expectations. They often take the form of a coach, a boss, a teacher, a mentor, or a leader—someone close enough to you to see your potential and really care, but far enough to have a balanced perspective. That distance also allows you to accept their honest feedback in a way you never could with someone very close to you. A best friend, parent, or spouse can rarely serve in this role, because you're just too close to them emotionally to accept their feedback without having a strong reaction.

A Bar Raiser has a rock-solid belief in your success that usually exceeds your own. That's because your potential is constrained by your self-doubt and limiting beliefs, so your Bar Raiser can see that's possible for you better than you can. In your moments of doubt (when other people might quit), your Bar Raiser tells you to keep going and assures you that the voices of doubt in your head are wrong. Although this relationship can serve many functions, this is the most important one: bridging you across the gap of self-doubt. Their mentorship sets a tone of "don't bother with excuses because I know you can do this"—but always in a deeply caring way.

This trusting dynamic plays out over time as a loop:
- You doubt yourself and think about quitting.
- Your Bar Raiser intervenes to bridge you past self-doubt.
- You succeed and are thrilled by the result.
- You trust your Bar Raiser even more and become willing to take bigger risks with them.
- Over time you internalize the voice of your Bar Raiser.

Most people first experienced this kind of relationship with a childhood sports coach or a music teacher—someone who expected more from you than you thought possible and ended up being right. As an adult, this could be a boss or a mentor who takes a particular interest in you, challenging you to accelerate your growth.

Unfortunately, by itself, this one layer is not enough.

THE BUDDY

The second layer of accountability is a buddy. Broadly defined, this is a dyad, or a small group of just two people. Buddies are one of the most fundamentally misunderstood types of accountability. Buddy relationships often fail because they use their buddy check-ins as bad therapy sessions, complaining to each other and justifying each other's excuses. Sadly, this is why a buddy relationship done wrong can hurt far more than it helps.

A great example of buddies gone wrong is a gym buddy. Most gym buddy partnerships fail miserably. It's just too easy to call or text the other person and give some excuse for not going to the gym. Both parties are probably looking for a reason to quit anyway and welcome the excuse to bail out. By justifying each other's motive, neither party makes it to the gym, and both feel validated in their choice. They're letting each other off the hook.

But how could this buddy dynamic be modified to get the desired result? My client Todd found a simple solution. At the end of each gym session, he and his buddy Paolo give each other one of their gym shoes. This shoe swap changed the dynamic in one simple but meaningful way: if one buddy doesn't make it to the gym, the other buddy can't work out that day. That means that their resistance not only hurts their own results, but it hurts their buddy as well. For most people, this is enough to nudge them into the desired action.

This type of arrangement is the gold standard of buddy relationships: the "sink or swim" buddy format. "Sink or swim" buddies are just what they sound like: the two of you will succeed or fail together. This relationship intertwines your results with your buddy's to force you to penalize them if you penalize yourself. In a corporate setting, a good example is determining some portion of a person's bonus based on their buddy's results, not just their own. Another classic example of this is the battle buddy system in the

US military, where buddies are committed to helping each other in specific ways, in and out of combat.

I'll be the first to admit that this is a tricky dynamic to create and isn't viable in all cases, and therefore isn't common. But it's worth mentioning because, when done right, it sets the gold standard for how powerful a buddy relationship can be.

A more attainable form of buddy relationship is a "mirror buddy." A mirror buddy reflects your thought process and self-evaluation from an outsider's perspective. When you report your progress to your buddy, they act as a mirror to reflect what you're saying back to you. That gives you a space to externalize your thoughts and see your life through a neutral lens. Ideally, your buddy doesn't inject any emotion or opinion into the dialogue—they simply repeat back to you what they're hearing and seeing. If they ask a question, it's not the Socratic method in disguise; they genuinely aren't understanding what you're saying. Here's an actual mock buddy conversation from a workshop I gave on this topic:

Alice: This week was kind of a mess.

Pradeep: How so?

Alice: I got my big priority done, but my other work piled up and I'm stressing about that right now. And my kids are angry that I grounded them this week. It just feels like a mess.

Pradeep: Maybe I'm missing something, but if you let a lot of small things pile up so that you could get the most important thing done, isn't that a perfect example of triaging your tasks? And with your kids, it seems like they are angry with you because you enforced healthy boundaries and rules. That sounds like good parenting. Am I missing something?

Alice: No, I guess you're right. I can't think of anything I would do differently. I just feel really bad right now.

Pradeep: Understood. So if you wouldn't change anything you did this week, would you say that you won your week?

Alice: I mean, you're right. I guess I was expecting it to feel a certain way. But yeah, this week was actually a huge win.

Notice how powerful the transformation was for Alice here: she went from feeling like she had lost the week to realizing that she had won it in an incredibly short span of time. A mirror buddy helps you strip away the emotion and see yourself through another person's eyes. Her buddy achieves this by simply listening and repeating what he's hearing. In the process, he's helping Alice realize that she won the week after all.

The number one mistake people make in a buddy dynamic is overcomplicating the relationship. People try to be cheerleaders for their buddies, injecting forced positivity into the dynamic. Or they try to be coaches, injecting judgments and advice. Or worse, they cosign on their buddy's excuses, giving them tacit permission to underperform.

You can find a great buddy by reaching out to your professional network or any community where you're an established member. In my Lifehack Tribe membership community, I host a monthly event called Accountability Buddy Speed Dating. It's essentially a networking event where members of the Tribe can quickly meet dozens of potential buddies all at once. But even if you're not part of a group that makes finding a buddy frictionless, I guarantee that there's someone in your network who would be thrilled by the idea of having you as an accountability buddy.

THE TEAM

The third layer is a team of people you respect. These are like-minded individuals in the same boat as you are, pushing toward similar goals. They are preferably at your level or higher in whatever game you're playing, because team accountability works best when you respect the people around you. That means that when they offer you support or feedback, it means something to you because you value their opinion highly.

But the best part of being on a team is the competition! If you're reading this book, chances are that you're a highly competitive person. Groups effortlessly amplify that competitive instinct. This friendly competition is extremely helpful in getting you to take action when you are fearful or resistant because competition can mask or outweigh fear.

When I was thirteen years old, my brothers, our friends, and I hiked to a waterfall in Hawaii. My older brother raced to jump off the top, followed by my other brother. I have an intense fear of heights. Despite that, I raced to the top to jump off before any of our friends did. Why? Because I knew that my friends would eventually jump, and I didn't want to be the last person to jump. The social pressure was instant and powerful, overcoming my evolutionary instinct to keep my feet planted safely on the ground.

I see this same dynamic in my coaching all the time. My most intensive program is an eight-week productivity bootcamp called Lifehack Bootcamp, where we essentially do eight years of productivity work in eight weeks. To achieve that rapid transformation, we have to push people far outside their comfort zone, often encountering stiff resistance. But we've also designed the program to amplify people's competitive instincts to overcome that resistance.

I had a client in one of my bootcamps who was a CEO of a multimillion dollar company. He hit a wall of resistance and insisted that he couldn't do what I was asking of him. In his mind, it just wasn't possible. I knew that it was, but I also knew that I couldn't appeal to his logic brain since he had decided to resist; I had to leverage social pressure. In that same bootcamp, there was also a lower-level executive succeeding in that same area where the CEO was faltering. All I had to do was point out to the CEO that someone he considered below him in the pecking order was getting a better result than he was. As quick as lightning, he dropped the excuses, did the work, and got the result. His competitive drive proved to be far stronger than his resistance and excuses.

Teams help us stop feeling sorry for ourselves and get in the game. Friendly competition is good, and there is enormous power if you can leverage it in the right way. You'll find an endless supply of motivation and discipline when you're on a team that pushes you.

PUBLIC ACCOUNTABILITY

The fourth layer is public accountability. Public accountability is when you have committed to a result publicly, and you know that you will be held accountable in a public forum.

A great example of this is a sports team. Everyone knows when the game is happening, and they watch it live. After the game, your win or loss gets splashed across the front page of the local newspaper. There's a lot of personal pride riding on the outcome, and there's nowhere to hide if you lose. This forum provides potent social heat. The pressure's on!

Sadly, most people lack opportunities for public accountability in their day-to-day life. If you don't write that book you've been wanting to write, usually no one finds out. We just quietly bury the bodies of our failures (I'll be the first to raise my hand and say I've been guilty of that one!). That's why I would advise you to *create* opportunities for public accountability.

Whenever we launch a new course, Carey and I advertise it before we've even created it and start taking people's money in pre-sales. That provides inescapable public accountability. People have paid for the course, and they expect it to be ready on the date we promised. The consequence of missing that date is unthinkable for us. People would say, "You are ripping us off! You promised it by this date and didn't deliver!" There's no better accountability for us, and we've moved mountains and performed minor miracles to launch on time.

My client Ash is a web designer. He beat out his competition on a big deal by guaranteeing the client that they would launch on a specific date—or they wouldn't pay a dime. In place of the future website, he had a countdown timer to the launch date. He told me, "I've never been more productive in my life! That countdown timer haunted my dreams."

This technique can even work for personal goals. My client Dita committed to a weight loss challenge that asked her to post photos of herself in just a sports bra every week for two months. She said, "You better believe I stuck to my diet...I knew I had that photo coming up on Sunday!"

The Four Layers of Accountability

- Bar Raiser
- Team
- Buddy
- Public

Those are four layers of accountability. Think about a time when you accomplished something extraordinary in your life—a time when you amazed yourself and exceeded what you thought was possible. You will usually realize you had two or more of these layers in your life, reinforcing your willpower and preventing you from wiggling out.

As you look to win your week, I want you to layer accountability into your life to amplify your discipline and motivation, preferably in a way that boosts your intrinsic motivation. While you don't need all four layers to achieve results, I encourage you to build in as many as possible. Like a fabric, more layers make for stronger, more durable accountability.

At its core, the secret to success with the Lifehack Method has been our commitment to creating these four layers of accountability for our clients. This simple concept has set us apart in a crowded coaching space and contributed to a 145 percent compound annual growth rate over the last six years. Now that you know about the layers of accountability, you can create them in any area where you want to achieve outsized results in your life—like productivity, fitness, or even learning to play the guitar.

CHAPTER RECAP

When you're working by yourself in a silo, you will inevitably succumb to resistance and excuses. Creating more willpower is not the answer to taking massive action and winning your weeks. Instead of growing your willpower to swim against the current, you want to change the flow of the current so that you can swim with it. Accountability can dramatically change that equation, reinforce your discipline, and generate motivation that feels like it's coming from inside you.

In this chapter we showed you the Four Layers of Accountability so you can wrap several interlacing layers around yourself. That's going to create an inescapable environment that prevents you from wiggling out in your weaker moments. If done properly, it could also boost intrinsic motivation, eliciting your best performance. You can download the Four Layers of Accountability PDF at **winningtheweek.com/resources**.

That's not to say there is no place for willpower. Willpower is like an index finger: incredibly important for detailed work, but not the strongest part of your body. If you need to push a car or pick up a log, it's not the right tool for the job. In the next chapter, I'll show you how to sharpen your mindsets and develop grit and determination to win your week.

13

DEBUG YOUR MINDSETS

BRITTANY PULLED INTO THE DRIVEWAY OF HER HOUSE IN UPPER Michigan, turned off the car, and started gathering her things. Out of nowhere, she started crying and didn't stop for fifteen minutes. She later told me, "I wasn't crying about anything in particular—it was just everything."

Maybe it was because Brittany was a mother of five children, caring for her own mother who had advanced Alzheimer's disease, and (since her husband had lost his job in the pandemic) she was now the breadwinner of the family. She said, "It's just all too much! There aren't enough hours in the week. I don't even have time to go to the bathroom." (She also dropped a couple of choice expletives that I'm leaving out.)

Fast-forward three weeks.

When Brittany and I talked next, I felt like I was talking to a different person. She was relaxed and happy. She told me she had just finished her second workout that week, a hobby she had been forced to give up years ago. She had cleared out her backlog of work and was heading into the weekend with nothing but free time. She told me about her plans to spend quality time with her teenage daughter and go golfing with her husband. She beamed as she told me, "This is Brittany 2.0. I feel like a new woman!"

What could explain such a dramatic transformation in that short period of time? Brittany had done the hard work to reconsider one of her most sinister limiting truths: "There's not enough time."

LIMITING TRUTHS AND HIGHER TRUTHS

What is a limiting truth? It's a belief that's undeniably true, yet it traps you in your current situation. It does so because you don't bother trying to solve a problem you're convinced is unsolvable. In Brittany's case, her limiting truth was "there's not enough time to get everything done." That was undoubtedly true because there was more to do than she had time to do it. But it was also a dead end. What was she supposed to do with that statement? Did she want to keep on going like she was? Certainly not! She called me because she was in pain and looking for a solution.

The problem with limiting truths is that they don't offer solutions. Worse, they convince you that the problem isn't solvable at all! That's why limiting truths are highly damaging to your productivity and can be a tremendous roadblock to winning your week. But there are versions of the truth that are far more productive. I call these "higher truths." Higher truths are just as true as limiting truths, but they point us toward a solution, and in the process, challenge us to step up to a higher level.

Let's go back to Brittany, crying in her car weeks earlier. I explained the idea of limiting truths to Brittany and asked her if she wanted to find a higher truth to escape this way of living. She eagerly said yes, and I challenged her to read—in the next forty-eight hours—the book *I Know How She Does It* by Laura Vanderkam. This book is an underappreciated masterpiece in the productivity genre. Vanderkam tracked busy, successful moms for years, carefully analyzing how they spent their time. Ultimately, Vanderkam discovered the secret of how they're able to "have it all"—success, family, and fulfillment.

I call it a masterpiece because Vanderkam accomplished something truly rare: her book shifts the reader from a limiting truth to a higher truth. People begin reading the book thinking, *There's not enough time in the day.*

By the end of the book, she's convinced them beyond a shadow of a doubt of a higher truth:

"There is enough time to get the important things done *if* I take radical ownership of my time!"

Vanderkam accomplished this feat by sharing story after story of career women (managers, entrepreneurs, small business owners) who took extreme ownership of their time and lived highly fulfilling lives. To build an unimpeachable case, she kept hourly time logs on those women for 1,001 days, creating a dataset to prove her point quantitatively as well as qualitatively. It all pointed to the same higher truth: there is enough time if you choose to take extreme ownership of it.

For Brittany, this small shift was like a dam bursting. Once she let go of her limiting truth and adopted this higher truth, she was able to change her circumstances within weeks. She dove into time tracking with gusto, relishing the opportunity to find out where she was losing or squandering time, and discovered ways to optimize and create more time. Here's what she found:

- She realized she was spending eight hours a week on social media.
- She cut activities that didn't create value or weren't appreciated.
- Unable to afford house help, she paid her kids to help run the household.
- Instead of resenting her husband, she gave him specific roles where he could help, along with detailed directions (clarity he had been craving for a long time).
- She enlisted her sister to start helping care for her ailing mother.

Within weeks Brittany's life had transformed, but the moment the dam broke was when she shifted her limiting truth to a higher truth.

THE LIMITING PRODUCTIVITY MINDSETS

The mindsets we adopt are like the software we run internally. I like to think of a limiting mindset as a bug in our software, jamming up the works and crashing our operating systems. Sometimes all it takes to get the program running is fixing one line of code. Fixing those broken lines of code can clean up your operating system and get it working like new. That's why breaking through those limiting truths is highly leveraged.

Coaching thousands of people in their productivity game has allowed me to scout out the most common limiting mindsets. I've identified nine archetypal limiting truths that hold people back from winning their week. As you're exploring them, I want you to focus on the limiting truths that feel the most unshakable to you, because those are likely the ones that are keeping you trapped. Like Brittany, simply shifting them to their higher truth can create incredible possibilities for you.

Let's review the most common limiting truths and their corresponding higher truths.

1. Limiting Truth: "I don't have enough hours in the day!"

We've all thought this one, right? It's a trap we all get snared in because it can certainly feel undeniably true. The kernel of truth inside is, yes, you have more things on your task list than time to do them. But it's also a trap because it doesn't give you any leads on how to solve the problem. Once you believe this limiting truth, you're stuck in a victim relationship with your time supply, accepting that you're powerless to make a change.

The higher truth is that there *is* enough time to get the important things accomplished, but only if you take extreme ownership of your time. When I have clients track their time, they never fail to discover pockets of unused and underutilized time. Having taken extreme ownership of your time, you even may find that you have enough time to get your wish list accomplished, with time to spare! But be warned: your capacity to add things to your task list outstrips your available resources. If that happens, go back to the chapters on triage and prioritizing with leverage. That's going to get you the most "bang for your buck" and make your life and work progressively easier.

2. Limiting Truth: "I just can't stay focused. There must be something wrong with me."

There's a kernel of truth here—every brain is different, and some of us have more trouble focusing than others. It's human nature to wonder if this is "just how I am," especially if you've struggled with focus for a long time. But once you tell yourself that this is an unshakable feature of your brain, you fall into a victim story. You relinquish any power you might have to change it. That's a limiting truth because it doesn't offer you a way forward.

The higher truth is that focus is more about your environment than it is about you, and there is a lot you can control and change in your environment. In the previous chapter, we discussed how our environment is more effective than our willpower in influencing behavior. When you shift this belief, you begin to notice all of the ways that you can work to create an enhanced environment that brings out your best performance—and that includes improving your ability to focus. It might take time and experimentation, but I've never had a client who didn't see improvement pursuing this higher truth.

3. Limiting Truth: "I've just got too much on my plate."

If the first limiting truth was that time supply was unfairly constrained, this one is the inverse: there's too much demand! It has a ring of truth to it because it's likely that you have put too much on your plate. But again, this thought traps you and places you in a victim posture. Let's get real: no matter how excellent you are at triaging your tasks, and no matter how aggressively you employ my TACO method, your task list will outpace your capacity to finish it. Accepting that hard truth means letting go of the idea that success means getting everything done. We need a new definition of success.

The higher truth here is that *success isn't about getting everything done. It's about getting the right things done, at the right time, in the right way.*

David Allen, the author of *Getting Things Done*, calls this the "martial art of getting things done." Inspired by martial arts, Allen thinks the best outcomes happen when we achieve maximal impact with minimal effort. We all know what it feels like to have a week where we get things done, but they weren't the right things. That results in the worst possible outcome: maximal effort and minimal impact, like Popeye winding up for a punch but missing his target completely! Those are the weeks when we are exhausted and have nothing to show for it. But when we choose the right leveraged priority, we can take comfort in knowing that we tackled the right thing and effected the maximum impact (no matter how crazy the week was).

The second part of that truth is more subtle: "at the right time." I've seen clients work on something too early, neglecting other work that needed their attention and would have had a higher impact. But far more often, I see clients work on things too late. This habit of always tackling things too late not only reduces the quality of your work but forces you to pay a far higher price in time, resources, and stress. I call this the "stupid tax," or the extra cost you pay dealing with things that you could (and should) have tackled earlier. The optimal timeline is in the "Goldilocks" zone: not too early and not too late.

I find the last part of that sentence is the hardest for people to grasp: "in the right way." The right way could mean a couple of things. It could mean achieving the right level of completion. Often my clients get overtaken by perfectionism, turning a one-hour task into a multiday "Mona Lisa" project. Finding the right level of completion means pausing to ask yourself, "Does this really need to be perfect, or does 'good enough' work here?" But the "right way" could also refer to your use of strategy and tactics. Is the way you're solving the problem the optimal route to success? This thought invites you to step back periodically and take a longer view. Sometimes that pause is all it takes to realize that there's a much better way to make the desired impact.

In sum, there's no such thing as getting everything done these days. But using this higher truth, you'll be able to feel good about your actions even when you finish the week with important things left on your task list.

4. Limiting Truth: "I don't control my time/money/priorities/schedule."

This one is common when you have a lot of competing responsibilities and you're trying to meet all of them simultaneously. Invariably, you'll twist yourself into a pretzel to make it work—and the result is feeling like a prisoner in your life. No one is asking for your opinion; they're just expecting you to satisfy their needs. It's easy to see why you might start to believe that you *are* a slave to your responsibilities and the people around you. But again, that puts you in a victim posture when it comes to your key resources—and nothing good comes from that. As a coach, I know I'm talking to someone like this when I make suggestions to improve, and they relentlessly respond:

- "My boss would never let me _____."
- "My team would never let me _____."
- "My company culture would never let me _____."
- "My wife would never let me _____."
- "My kids would never let me _____."

The higher truth is that **your ownership of your key resources is inalienable. It can't be given up without your consent**. (Key resources include your time, your energy, your money, etc.)

My client Noah was a great example of this in action. When I suggested he triage his tasks and employ leverage to push his agenda forward, he told me, "I can't set my own priorities because my boss keeps taking me off track. And he's in charge at the end of the day." What he's really saying is, "I don't control my priorities. My boss does." Believing this to be true, Noah ignored my advice and continued to fight fires for his boss, to the detriment of his own progress. At his year-end review, Noah's boss told him he had failed to hit the target they had assigned him and would not be awarded a bonus for that year. Noah felt violated, telling his boss that the reason he didn't hit his targets was that he was doing the things that his boss had told him to. His boss replied, "It's not my job to defend your priorities. You have to push back and fight for the agenda you've been assigned to lead." As infuriating as that sounds, his boss was actually right.

The irony of life is that we can run ourselves into the ground trying to do everything people ask of us, yet somehow fail to recognize their greatest needs and meet them. After the sting had worn off, I told Noah:

"You weren't hired to follow orders. You were hired to create positive outcomes in the best way you know how, using the resources you have. Your boss don't be expected to know the best use of your time—you have to fight to show him what that is. As a professional, you have earned the right to allocate your resources in the way you see fit and be judged by the results."

This limiting mindset isn't just about work either. You don't get married to become a servant to the other person's every whim. You get to decide how to fulfill your wedding vows in the best way you see fit, using the resources you have at hand. Taking back ownership of your key resources isn't going to be easy, especially if you've trained everyone around you to think of you as a "whipping boy." But once people see that their core needs are being met in a better way, they'll start to trust you.

Not to be morbid, but when it comes time to pass on from this life, you won't be able to blame anyone else for the things you did or didn't do. Saying, "I didn't live my life the way I wanted, because so-and-so wouldn't let me" sounds like a pretty pathetic way to go.

5. Limiting Truth: "This imperfect ___ is keeping me from results."

This one refers to the "if onlys" of life. People get obsessed with a crystal clear vision of what life *should be*. I call this vision the "perfect solution." They have a picture in their head of how things could go perfectly—if only life would cooperate with their plans! This vision is funny because if life has one consistent quality, it's that it doesn't cooperate with anyone's plans. Despite this, we still develop strong expectations around our perfect solutions, which are then promptly dashed. Crestfallen, we use this as an excuse to play the victim:

- "I could have been on time if only I hadn't hit traffic!"
- "I could have stuck to my diet if only it hadn't been the holidays."
- "I could have quit smoking if only my wife had quit too."

- "We could have hit the deadline if only that last-minute emergency hadn't popped up!"

The higher truth is that there are zero perfect solutions and infinite imperfect solutions.

Modern life is inherently chaotic, and it's your job to navigate a path through those churning waters. They aren't going to part for you like they did for Moses and offer you a clear, uncontested pathway. Life will not cooperate with your vision of a perfect solution. Instead, you get to start looking at all the imperfect solutions. Imperfect solutions are the ones that concede to the chaos of life and participate anyway. For example, leaving early to get to your destination isn't ideal because it risks wasting your time. It's an imperfect solution that concedes to reality and ensures that you get the desired result (making it to that appointment on time), even if things go sideways.

The good news is that you can choose from many imperfect solutions. While there is only one perfect solution, there are infinite imperfect solutions to every problem. While your ideal solution rarely works out, you'll find that imperfect solutions perfectly fit your imperfect reality. (Wrap your head around that sentence!)

6. Limiting Truth: "I can't focus or motivate because I'm so worried about [an external situation out of my control]."

This one is so pervasive today because there are so many things to worry about! The political climate, the morality of the younger generation, whether or not you'll close that business deal, if things will "work out"—the list goes on and on. The problem with worrying about situations outside your control is that you can't possibly affect the outcome, so every bit of energy expended on it is *wasted*.

The higher truth comes by asking yourself, "What's the optimal level of thinking and caring about this that can positively affect the situation?"

I am personally prone to this limiting truth, and I have to fight it again and again when it comes up. One of my worst qualities is that I'm a recovering news junky, and my addiction has been (in the past) following political news. If unchecked, I will go down the rabbit hole, tracking daily updates and obsessing over every blow-by-blow. The problem is that this was a massive waste of my time, given that the president wasn't calling me on a red phone to ask me my opinion on the political fight of the day. Worse, it got me extremely anxious and frustrated, which had a negative impact on my quality of life, my family's experience of me, and even my business. All of that energy, and all of that time, didn't alter the situation one iota.

I asked myself what (if anything) I could do to affect the outcome, and I realized I had already done it: I had voted. The point of representative democracy is that I had nominated *someone else* to engage the messy political process so that I could remain focused on my life and my business. So I decided to stop following the day-to-day updates and not let them consume any more of my cognitive energy. You can probably guess what happened: to my everlasting shock, the political world did not notice that I had stopped paying attention, and I got my time, sanity, and mental health back.

If you think about it, you can probably come up with dozens of situations in your life where you are expending mental energy that is not changing the outcome. Your best choice is to refocus that energy or give the situation the minimum level of attention needed to effect a positive change.

7. Limiting Truth: "The stakes are so high that I'm freaking out!"

I find that, around the college years, you start realizing that your performance has real consequences. If you don't ace the interview, you won't get the job. If you have a bad day on the court, you'll lose the championship. Once you start gaining responsibilities in life, those high-stakes moments can begin to mess with your mental game.

But ironically, the higher the stakes of the game, the more you need to stay calm and loose. When you tense up, this affects your performance negatively. Of course, practice helps with this, so the more you can prepare for the big moment, the better off you'll be. But when the moment comes, the best thing to do is stay loose and play it like a game.

That's why the higher truth here is to **play it like a game and try to enjoy yourself**. If unchecked, life can get too serious. But it's important to remember how few real consequences there are in the grand scheme of things. Most of us are not facing down a lion in the savanna, where one wrong move carries a death sentence. Failure—in our plush, spoiled modern world—isn't really failure at all. In practically every area of life, we can restart the video game and play again.

So relax and try to enjoy yourself a little. Bring your attention back to the very next action: the next kick, the next throw. That's what high-stakes moments deserve because your best energy will shine through.

8. Limiting Truth: "It feels like life gets harder and harder every year."

If you're playing the game of life right, each win brings new responsibilities. I referred to this earlier in the book as the Conqueror's Curse, where every victory brings you more responsibilities to maintain and defend. So yes, life tends to get more challenging and complex as you progress. But that's not all that's changing. You're changing too. Each win and each failure is teaching you, helping you grow and adapt.

The higher truth is that it never gets easier, but you get better. Every time you win the week, you'll learn new lessons and forge yourself in the fire of experience. If you don't lose that desire to learn and grow stronger, you'll increase your ability to tolerate the stress of responsibility. Any parent with multiple kids will tell you that they barely got through the first child with their sanity intact, but by the time they got to the last one, they were having fun with it. The circumstances didn't change; if anything, their last child should have been more challenging because they had the most logistics to juggle at that point. What changed was their improved ability to handle the responsibilities.

9. Limiting Truth: "I can't be expected to play if I'm hurt."

There's no better excuse to play the victim than when you're genuinely hurt. That could be a physical hurt, like an injury or an illness, or it could be psychological pain, like a crisis or mental health moment. Regardless, the tendency is to run to the sidelines of your game and tap out. Nobody could blame you. To be clear, there are moments when it's not wise to keep playing: moments when there are no severe consequences on the line, and the benefit of playing hurt is far outweighed by the costs or risks. But there are also moments when—as the star player in the game of your life—your team needs you to play hurt and be the hero who pulls out the win.

The higher truth is that **you can give yourself permission to play hurt when the game is on the line**.

This small insight has been tremendous for me. Somehow, I expected that I should only have to work if I'm in tip-top shape. But on any given day, there's always *something* that ails me, physically or emotionally. Maybe I have a headache or I underslept the night before. If I waited to be in perfect shape to play my game, I wouldn't be a starting player.

CHAPTER RECAP

The mindsets you adopt are like the software you run internally. A limiting mindset is like a bug in your mental software, jamming up the works and crashing your operating system. That can present huge roadblocks to winning your weeks.

Limiting mindsets are so powerful because they are based on limiting truths that trap you in your current situation. You can't destroy a limiting truth, but you can replace it with a higher truth that points you toward a solution. Sometimes all it takes to get your operating system running again is fixing that one line of code. A slight shift can be the break in the dam that gives way to massive positive change.

In this chapter, I identified nine archetypal limiting truths that keep people from winning their week. I then placed them alongside their corresponding higher truths to make it easy for you to root them out. As you've seen, most of them are easily overcome with the right higher truth to take their place. Download a summary of all nine limiting mindsets and the corresponding higher truths at **winningtheweek.com/resources**.

If you find yourself stuck in a limiting truth—it's okay. They are bound to crop up every once in a while. But don't let them take root and spread. Find your way to the higher truth to avoid hitting dead ends. Once you know how to shift your mindset the moment those thoughts occur, you'll be well on your way to stepping back into ownership of your mind and your actions.

CONCLUSION

Those who are victorious plan effectively and change decisively. They are like a great river that maintains its course but adjusts its flow.

—SUN TZU

WHILE I'D LOVE TO SAY THAT THE WINNING THE WEEK METHOD is new, the wise thinkers of antiquity have pointed us to these ideas for centuries. We're only new messengers. And yet, in this age of digital distractions, the message is needed now more than ever.

Today's productivity world is dominated by fads and trends, not a common-sense approach. Whether by design or by accident, the constant blur of media doesn't leave us space to piece together a rational productivity philosophy. That blur keeps us looking for the "next thing," a need marketers are all too happy to fulfill. Eventually, the marketing deluge becomes indistinguishable from our internal monologue. The result is that instead of becoming more productive, we're becoming more confused.

Let us help you cut through that confusion: the surest path to winning your week is planning your week ahead of time, every single week. It's something everyone knows they should be doing, *but practically no one does.* Carey and I wrote this book to help the reader rediscover planning as if they were looking at it with fresh eyes, seeing it for the very first time.

Through that new lens, you can now see that planning a winning week is a deceptively hard thing to do. It requires letting go of fads and crazes. It means defeating internal resistance and creating a positive feedback loop. It asks you to have the courage to choose one priority at the expense of others. It forces you to go beyond the simple calendar review to actively interrogate your calendar and ruthlessly triage your tasks. It makes you match your time demand to your time supply, removing any space for magical thinking. And finally, it forces you to make tough decisions with eyes wide open to the consequences.

Then, as you follow your plan, winning the week requires that you let go of perfection and bring the mindset of a sailor, navigating a new direction even as winds unfairly blow you off course. You must engineer an environment of focus and build accountability into your life to buttress your weaker moments. Finally, you have to upgrade your mental operating system by working on your mindsets.

I hope you can see now why planning is so rare: it's not one skill but a combination of about eleven separate productivity skills. Like riding a bike, the trick is to practice these skills in concert until they merge into one experience—the experience of winning your week. Were we all supposed to figure that out on our own?

Carey and I have been refining The Winning The Week Method for years to create a simple system that enables you to do all of this in less than thirty minutes.

The Winning The Week Method

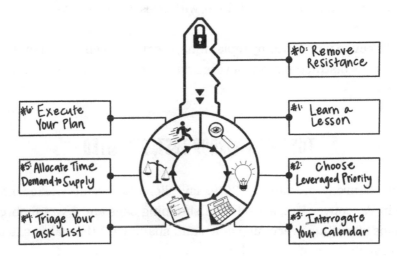

The Winning The Week Method shows you how to:

1. **Remove the resistance** that every adult has naturally built against planning, the natural result of the anxiety and fear it inflicts upon us. We showed you how to transform that resistance into craving.

2. **Learn a lesson each week,** creating a learning loop that allows for exponential improvement. Without this self-reflection, you will fall victim to making the same mistakes over and over.

3. **Choose a leveraged priority.** Avoid prioritizing what feels important and instead choose to prioritize the thing that makes your life consistently easier.

4. **Interrogate your calendar.** Go beyond the casual calendar review to interrogate your calendar, looking for landmines and wargaming your week. Remember that you have to beat your calendar up a little bit for it to tell you the truth.

5. **Triage your task list** ruthlessly to ensure that you're only considering the highest-yielding bids on your time. Remember that you have to be ruthless to do the most good!
6. **Allocate time demand to supply.** Make the tough choices about what's really going to get done, with eyes wide open to the consequences.
7. **Execute your plan** by replanning, creating an environment that blocks distractions, and leveraging the four layers of accountability.

THE FOYER MIRROR TEST, REVISITED

One Saturday morning in 2019, my client Catherine walked into her house in Vancouver B.C., arms full of shopping bags and a wet umbrella. In the chaos of putting everything down and shaking off the water, she looked up and caught herself in the mirror.

"I burst out laughing because I immediately thought of you and the Foyer Mirror Test," she told me, "It was silly and awkward, but it was enough to remind me to take a moment to reflect on my week. And you know what? I knew right away that I had won my week. I could feel it. Just being clear on that—and having a plan already in place for next week—I had probably the most restful weekend since before my kids were born. So I have to give it to you, Demir. I was a skeptic, but it works."

The Winning The Week Method helps you win the week, every week. Rather than take my word for it, why not try it yourself? Your test of success is simple: Take the Foyer Mirror Test each Friday. When you come in the door, don't rush past that mirror. Take a pause to look at yourself and ask the critical question: "Did I win the week, or did I lose it?" I'm confident that by employing this method, you'll look at yourself, smile through tired eyes, and say, "I crushed it!"

Then why not treat yourself like the returning hero? Put work aside and eagerly embrace the people you love so dearly. Blast your favorite playlist and pour yourself a drink. Take a celebratory sip and get closure on the week, allowing yourself to disengage and deeply relax. After all, what's the point of winning the battle if you can't enjoy the spoils of war?

If you're ready for that ride, pull out your laptop now and schedule a recurring appointment every Friday night or Saturday morning to pre-plan your week. You can even plan alongside your coworkers, life partner, or friends if they're willing. You have everything you need in these pages, but we've also included helpful supplementary trainings, cheat sheets, and PDF downloads—all free online at **winningtheweek.com/resources**.

Have you planned your week this week?

Tag @demirandcarey so we can celebrate with you!

Once you've applied these concepts and are convinced they work, we would be so grateful if you passed this information along to the people around you. Of course we'd be honored if you recommended this book so that the people in your life can learn these concepts too. But you can also start by teaching people around you. Even children can grasp this method in simplified form. (I'd love to live in a world where our kids don't struggle with productivity like we did, wouldn't you?)

The next time you hear someone obsessing over the newest productivity fad taking our culture by storm, ask them how many times they planned their week in the last month. If the answer isn't "every single week," rest assured that you're not missing out on anything.

ACKNOWLEDGMENTS

READER, WE'D LIKE TO THANK YOU SINCERELY FOR READING THIS book to the end; we know it's a significant expenditure of time and energy. Hopefully, you'll find that what you've learned will pay off huge dividends in your life and will give you all of that time back and more.

A huge thank you goes out to our entire Lifehack Method community, filled with Lifehackers who put this work into action every day and inspire us to no end. Many people falsely assume that all of our knowledge comes from our own experience. In truth, we've learned lifetimes of lessons by working with thousands of clients in hundreds of industries over almost a decade. This book is a victory for our whole community, which is collectively dedicated to finding the most straightforward and powerful ways of operating.

A special thank you to our incredible illustrator, Harlee Keller. Since week one, Harlee has been with our Lifehack Method team. We are so thankful for her creative talent, project management skills, and willingness to tackle new projects with positivity and enthusiasm. Thank you also to our skilled graphic designer, Laura Patricelli, who whipped up a fantastic book cover we loved the moment we saw it.

We also want to thank our beloved team members, especially Aiden McFarland, Kendra Beery, Sarah Skedd, Kevin Loder, Sierra Montoya, and Jessica Lackey for representing Lifehack Method values day in and day out and making our company better every week.

Special thanks to Enver Gjokaj for stepping in to be our de facto editor. You helped us hash out ideas with passion and excitement, tolerated late-night brainstorming sessions, and contributed excellent insights to the concepts in the book. You're an exceptional communicator, and we're lucky to have you in our corner.

Thank you to our publicist, Selena Soo, and her team, and to publisher Scribe Media for believing in our mission and helping us champion this message to as many people as possible.

And finally, this book was vastly improved by the energy, passion, and insight from fifty of our clients who took the time to read early drafts and give feedback—especially Sarah Skedd, Lenora Biemans, JoAnn Carollo, Kathryn Read, Bruce Fleck, Raelynn Steffensmeier, Wael Masri, Jessica Lackey, Darleen Ghirardi, Tecca Wright, Javier Paz, Jill Rosenthal, Janna Willard, Adam Finer, Erich Ball, Shaloo Savla, Veronika Ambertson, Kari Valcourt, Jesse Markowitz, Margie Barrie, Tim Burns, Kerry Madden, Eric Bean, Gabrielle Islwyn, Christian Georg Hirschbiel, Jessica Snyder, David Washbrook, Shariff Dinah, Andrea Aal, Eric Bean, Sean Hogan, Jennifer Rade, Tiffany Brandt, Guy Porter, and Sandra Park. Thank you so much.

NOTES

INTRODUCTION

It's estimated that 24 million people: "About Autoimmunity," The American Autoimmune Related Diseases Association, March 11, 2022, https://autoimmune.org/resource-center/about-autoimmunity/.

In a massive thirty-year study: H. Huan Song, F. Fang, G. Tomasson et al., "Association of Stress-Related Disorders with Subsequent Autoimmune Disease," *JAMA* 319, no. 23 (2018): 2388–2400, https://jamanetwork.com/journals/jama/article-abstract/2685155/.

Sudden occupational mortality: Tsutomu Hoshuyama, Satoru Saeki, Ken Takahashi, and Toshiteru Okubo, "A Descriptive Epidemiology on Sudden Death among Workers," *Journal of UOEH* 14, no. 3 (1992): 219–225, https://pubmed.ncbi.nlm.nih.gov/1410940/.

Jory MacKay, "The 9–5 Workday Is Dead: New Research Shows 92% of People Work on Evenings and Weekends (even before the pandemic),"

RescueTime, May 20, 2020, https://blog.rescuetime.com/work-life-balance-survey-2020-2/.

A UK study of the impacts on family life: Shirley Dex, "Families and Work in the Twenty-First Century," Joseph Rowntree Foundation, September 2, 2003, https://www.jrf.org.uk/report/families-and-work-twenty-first-century.

400 percent more productive than a worker was in 1950: "Nonfarm Business Sector: Labor Productivity (Output per Hour) for All Employed Persons," FRED, March 3, 2022, https://fred.stlouisfed.org/series/OPHNFB.

G. E. Miller, "The US Is the Most Overworked Developed Nation in the World," 20 Something Finance, January 30, 2022, https://20somethingfinance.com/american-hours-worked-productivity-vacation/.

Greg Daugherty, "History of the Cost of Living," Investopedia, July 14, 2021, https://www.investopedia.com/ask/answers/101314/what-does-current-cost-living-compare-20-years-ago.asp.

"I know kung fu.": This line is spoken by Neo, played by Keanu Reeves, in *The Matrix*, directed by Lilly and Lana Wachowski (1999).

CHAPTER 1: WHY WIN THE WEEK?

Hans Selye, "Confusion and Controversy in the Stress Field," *Journal of Human Stress* 1, no. 2 (1975): 37–44, https://pubmed.ncbi.nlm.nih.gov/1235113/.

"Work expands so as to fill the time": British naval historian and author Cyril Northcote Parkinson wrote that opening line for an essay in *The Economist* in 1955, but the concept known as "Parkinson's law" still lives on today. "Parkinson's Law," *The Economist*, November 19, 1955, **https://www.economist.com/news/1955/11/19/parkinsons-law/**.

CHAPTER 2: THE WINNING THE WEEK METHOD

"Give me six hours to chop down a tree": Though widely attributed to Abraham Lincoln, this quote has unclear provenance. Here's a resource that takes a skeptical view: "To Cut Down a Tree in Five Minutes Spend Three

Minutes Sharpening Your Axe," Quote Investigator, March 29, 2014, https://quoteinvestigator.com/2014/03/29/sharp-axe/.

"Plans are worthless. But planning is indispensable": Though Dwight D. Eisenhower did say this many times, it was likely adapted from a military adage: "Plans Are Worthless, But Planning Is Everything," Quote Investigator, November 18, 2017, https://quoteinvestigator.com/2017/11/18/planning/.

Limbic system (also known as your "lizard brain"): Joseph Troncale, "Your Lizard Brain," *Psychology Today*, April 22, 2014, https://www.psychologytoday.com/intl/blog/where-addiction-meets-your-brain/201404/your-lizard-brain/.

Mere Urgency Effect: Meng Zhu, Yang, and Christopher K. Hsee, "The Mere Urgency Effect," *Journal of Consumer Research* 45, no. 3 (2018): 673–690, https://doi.org/10.1093/jcr/ucy008/.

CHAPTER 3: REMOVE THE RESISTANCE

Limbic system can go haywire: For more on how our bodies respond to stress, see "Understanding the Stress Response," *Harvard Health Publishing*, July 6, 2020, https://www.health.harvard.edu/staying-healthy/understanding-the-stress-response/; Kimberly Holland, "Amygdala Hijack: When Emotion Takes Over," *Healthline*, September 17, 2021, https://www.healthline.com/health/stress/amygdala-hijack/.

Logic brain: While the mechanics of brain functioning are complex and not wholly understood, logic brain is used in this book to describe the world of brain processes that result in logical, rational, and bias-free conclusions. Gerald L. Clore, "Psychology and the Rationality of Emotion," *Modern Theology* 27, no. 2 (2011): 325–338, https://www.ncbi.nlm.nih.gov/pmc/articles/PMC4128497/.

"Digital nomad": Digital nomads are people who are location-independent and use technology to perform their job, living a nomadic lifestyle. Adam Hayes, "What Is a Digital Nomad?" Investopedia, July 27, 2021, **https://www.investopedia.com/terms/d/digital-nomad.asp/**.

"Kodak moment": An occasion suitable for memorializing with a photograph; 1980s, from Kodak, the proprietary name of a photography company.

Lexico (Oxford University Press, 2022), https://www.lexico.com/definition/kodak_moment.

Trader Joe's: An American chain of grocery stores, https://www.trader-joes.com/home/.

These environments generate serotonin, oxytocin: Juan C. Brenes, Jaime Fornaguera, and **Andrey Sequeira-Cordero**, "Environmental Enrichment and Physical Exercise Attenuate the Depressive-Like Effects Induced by Social Isolation Stress in Rats," *Frontiers in Pharmacology*, May 29, 2020, https://www.frontiersin.org/articles/10.3389/fphar.2020.00804/full/.

CHAPTER 4: CREATE A POSITIVE FEEDBACK LOOP

"Deliberate practice": K. Anders Ericsson, Ralf Th. Krampe, and Clemens Tesch-Romer, "The Role of Deliberate Practice in the Acquisition of Expert Performance," *Psychological Review* 100, no. 3 (1993): 363–406, https://graphics8.nytimes.com/images/blogs/freakonomics/pdf/DeliberatePractice(PsychologicalReview).pdf/.

Benjamin Franklin: K. Anders Ericsson, Michael J. Prietula, and Edward T. Cokely, "The Making of an Expert," *Harvard Business Review*, July–August 2007, https://hbr.org/2007/07/the-making-of-an-expert/.

***Groundhog Day* with Bill Murray:** A self-centered Pittsburgh weatherman finds himself inexplicably trapped in a small town as he lives the same day over and over again. Directed by Harold Ramis, 1993, https://www.imdb.com/title/tt0107048/.

Negativity bias: Amrisha Vaish, Tobias Grossmann, and Amanda Woodward, "Not All Emotions Are Created Equal: The Negativity Bias in Social-Emotional Development," *Psychological Bulletin Journal* 134, no. 3 (2008): 383–403, https://pubmed.ncbi.nlm.nih.gov/18444702/.

CHAPTER 5: CHOOSE THE RIGHT PRIORITY

"If everything is important, then nothing is important.": Garr Reynolds, author of **Presentation Zen**, was referencing ways to consider what to include in presentations. **"What is the one thing you can do such**

that, by doing it, everything else will be easier or unnecessary?": Gary Keller and Jay Papasan, *The One Thing: The Surprisingly Simple Truth Behind Extraordinary Results* (Portland: Bard Press, 2013).

"Switching costs": "Multitasking: Switching Costs," American Psychological Association, March 20, 2006, https://www.apa.org/research/action/multitask/; Glenn Wylie and Alan Allport, "Task Switching and the Measurement of 'Switch Costs,'" *Psychological Research*, 63, nos. 3–4 (2000): 212–233, https://pubmed.ncbi.nlm.nih.gov/11004877/.

Classic definition of a lever: "Moments, Levers and Gears," BBC, https://www.bbc.co.uk/bitesize/guides/ztjpb82/revision/3/.

Ants can lift up to five thousand times their own body weight: Vienny Nguyen, Blaine Lilly, and Carlos Castro, "The Exoskeletal Structure and Tensile Loading Behavior of an Ant Neck Joint," *Journal of Biomechanics* 47, no. 2 (2014): 497–504, https://www.sciencedirect.com/science/article/pii/S0021929013005459/.

Mandy's mind went blank: Mia Belle Frothingham, "Fight, Flight, Freeze, or Fawn: What This Response Means," Simply Psychology, October 6, 2021, https://www.simplypsychology.org/fight-flight-freeze-fawn.html/.

CHAPTER 6: INTERROGATE YOUR CALENDAR

One small Italian white truffle can retail for $211: "Truffle Price Tracker," Truffle Farm, accessed April 18, 2021, https://truffle.farm/truffle_prices.html/.

A truffle starts losing its signature odor in just five days: Dominic Peterson, "How Long Does Truffle Last? Expiration Explained," Dom Eats, September 24, 2021, https://www.domeats.com/how-long-does-truffle-last/.

Premeditatio malorum: Igor Jankovic, "What is 'Premeditatio Malorum'?" The Wise Mind, September 15, 2020, https://thewisemind.net/what-is-premeditatio-malorum/.

War-gaming: To plan or conduct in the manner of a war game, *Merriam Webster Dictionary*, https://www.merriam-webster.com/dictionary/war-game.

"Every battle is won before it is fought.": Sun Tzu, *The Art of War*, Goodreads, https://www.goodreads.com/quotes/720920-every-battle-is-won-before-it-s-ever-fought/

CHAPTER 7: TRIAGE YOUR TASK LIST

Horrid battle conditions: Charles J. Esdaile, *Napoleon's Wars: An International History 1803–1815* (New York: Penguin Group, 2008).

Modern system of triage: Panagiotis N. Skandalakis, et al., "'To Afford the Wounded Speedy Assistance': Dominique Jean Larrey and Napoleon," *World Journal of Surgery* 30, no. 8 (2006): 1392–1399, https://pubmed.ncbi.nlm.nih.gov/16850154/.

Triage is a classification system: *The Oxford Mini-Dictionary* (Oxford University Press, 1991), 567.

"Closing your open loops": David Allen, *Getting Things Done: The Art of Stress-Free Productivity* (New York: Viking, 2001).

"Someday Tasks": David Allen advises putting these tasks on what he calls a "Someday/Maybe List." "What Goes on the Maybe List," GTD, October 10, 2010, **https://gettingthingsdone.com/2010/10/what-goes-on-a-someday-maybe-list/.**

"I have two kinds of problems": When former US president Dwight D. Eisenhower said this in a 1954 speech to the Second Assembly of the World Council of Churches, he was quoting Dr. J. Roscoe Miller, president of Northwestern University. The "Eisenhower Principle" is said to be how he organized his workload and priorities. "Eisenhower's Urgent/Important Principle," Mind Tools, https://www.mindtools.com/pages/article/newHTE_91.htm/.

CHAPTER 8: ALLOCATE TIME DEMAND TO SUPPLY

Nir Eyal: *Indistractable: How to Control Your Attention and Choose Your Life* (Dallas: BenBella, 2019).

Experts say we should tell our money exactly where we want it to go.: "How to Manage Your Money," Ramsey Solutions, February 2, 2022, https://www.ramseysolutions.com/retirement/how-to-manage-your-money.

"Art of what's possible and attainable": Otto von Bismarck, GoodReads, **https://www.goodreads.com/quotes/424187-politics-is-the-art-of-the-possible-the-attainable/**.

"Long tail": (in retail and marketing) Used to refer to the large number of products that sell in small quantities, as contrasted with the small number of bestselling products. Lexico (Oxford University Press, 2022), https://www.lexico.com/en/definition/long_tail/.

CHAPTER 9: STICK TO YOUR PLAN

They were on a voyage across the Atlantic: Bert Kreischer, "Sailing La Vagabonde's Most Dangerous Trip—CLIP—Bertcast," YouTube, 15:09, https://www.youtube.com/watch?v=kaJikPiuEI0/.

Studies have shown that you slow down to produce less: John Pencavel, "The Productivity of Working Hours," *Economic Journal* 125, no. 589 (2014): 2052–2076, https://ftp.iza.org/dp8129.pdf/; Kabir Sehgal and Deepak Chopra, "Stanford Professor: Working This Many Hours a Week Is Basically Pointless. Here's How to Get More Done—By Doing Less," CNBC, March 21, 2019, https://www.cnbc.com/2019/03/20/stanford-study-longer-hours-doesnt-make-you-more-productive-heres-how-to-get-more-done-by-doing-less.html/.

Bonaparte notoriously instructed his secretary not to open letters for three weeks: Ralph Waldo Emerson, **"Napoleon, or The Man of the World."** In *Representative Men* (1850).

CHAPTER 10: STOP DISTRACTING YOURSELF

"Flow state": Mihaly Csikszentmihalyi, "Flow, the Secret to Happiness." Filmed in February 2004. TED Conference video, 18:42. https://www.ted.com/talks/mihaly_csikszentmihalyi_flow_the_secret_to_happiness/.

Distractions kill our productivity: Gloria Mark et al., "The Cost of Interrupted Work: More Speed and Stress," Department of Informatics University of California, Irvine, https://www.ics.uci.edu/~gmark/chi08-mark.pdf/.

Gamification: The application of typical elements of game playing (e.g., point scoring, competition with others, rules of play) to other areas of activity. Lexico (Oxford University Press, 2022), https://www.lexico.com/en/definition/gamification/.

CHAPTER 11: BLOCK EXTERNAL DISTRACTIONS

Focused state for just *three minutes and five seconds*: "Too Many Interruptions at Work?" Gallup, June 6, 2006, https://news.gallup.com/businessjournal/23146/too-many-interruptions-work.aspx/.

CHAPTER 12: DESIGN POWERFUL ACCOUNTABILITY

Elite runners had been looking to break that barrier since 1886: Bill Taylor, "What Breaking the 4-Minute Mile Taught Us about the Limits of Conventional Thinking," *Harvard Business Review*, March 9, 2018, https://hbr.org/2018/03/what-breaking-the-4-minute-mile-taught-us-about-the-limits-of-conventional-thinking/.

Social pressure: The exertion of influence on a person or group by another person or group. **APA Dictionary of Psychology**, https://dictionary.apa.org/social-pressure/.

"Enriched environments": Benjamin Hardy, *Willpower Doesn't Work: Discover the Hidden Keys to Success* (New York City: Hachette Books, 2019).

"Eustress": Hans Selye, "Confusion and Controversy in the Stress Field," *Journal of Human Stress* 1, no. 2 (1975): 37–44, https://pubmed.ncbi.nlm.nih.gov/1235113/.

CHAPTER 13: DEBUG YOUR MINDSETS

Laura Vanderkam, *I Know How She Does It: How Successful Women Make the Most of Their Time* (United Kingdom: Portfolio, 2015).

"Martial art of getting things done": David Allen, *Getting Things Done: The Art of Stress-Free Productivity* (New York: Viking, 2001).

A free ebook edition is available with the purchase of this book.

To claim your free ebook edition:

1. Visit MorganJamesBOGO.com
2. Sign your name CLEARLY in the space
3. Complete the form and submit a photo of the entire copyright page
4. You or your friend can download the ebook to your preferred device

Morgan James
BOGO™

A **FREE** ebook edition is available for you or a friend with the purchase of this print book.

CLEARLY SIGN YOUR NAME ABOVE

Instructions to claim your free ebook edition:
1. Visit MorganJamesBOGO.com
2. Sign your name CLEARLY in the space above
3. Complete the form and submit a photo of this entire page
4. You or your friend can download the ebook to your preferred device

Print & Digital Together Forever.

Snap a photo

Free ebook

Read anywhere